D1575865

Who Named the Daisy?
Who Named the Rose?

Who Named the Daisy?
Who Named the Rose?

A ROVING DICTIONARY OF
NORTH AMERICAN WILDFLOWERS

Mary Durant

DRAWINGS BY ELEANOR COONEY

DODD, MEAD & COMPANY · NEW YORK

Text copyright © 1976 by Mary Durant
Illustrations copyright © 1976 by Eleanor Cooney
All rights reserved
No part of this book may be reproduced in any form
without permission in writing from the publisher
Printed in the United States of America

Library of Congress Cataloging in Publication Data

Durant, Mary B
    Who named the daisy? Who named the rose?

    1. Plant lore—Dictionaries. 2. Plant names,
Popular—Dictionaries. 3. Wild flowers—North America.
I. Title.
QK83.D87   581'.03   76-22513
ISBN 0-396-07332-8

For my husband Michael Harwood

I have a rival in every bird.
He has a rival in every flower.

Introduction

This book began several years ago in a wet meadow in Maine, where I had picked a stalk of mitrewort, or bishop's hat, as it is sometimes known—a wildflower with starry white blossoms that grow in a slender spire. I knew the plant well. I had known its name for years. But the thought suddenly struck me, as I stood in the meadow with the flower in hand, that I had no idea why it was called mitrewort. There was nothing about the leaves or the blossoms that could possibly be described as ecclesiastical, nothing even faintly to suggest a bishop's mitre.

When I got home to my reference books, I scouted it down. The mystery was solved. The Latin name for mitrewort is *Mitella*, or "little cap," and it specifically describes the hat-like shape of the seed pod. No wonder it made no sense when I studied the leaves and the flowers under a magnifying glass. But the shape of the pod had inspired the choice of the name some three hundred years ago, when a French botanist, Joseph Pitton de Tournefort, received a specimen plant from the New World in the 1600's and studied it under his magnifying glass. Mitrewort and bishop's hat are the English versions of the Latin name with which de Tournefort dubbed the newly discovered flower.

With that, my project began. What about other common names for our wild plants. Who had chosen them? And why?

There are, of course, thousands upon thousands of common names for American wildflowers that need no translation. Once you know the plant in question, the source of its name is self-evident. The sunflower, cattail, lizard tail, blue-eyed grass, bluebell, spring beauty, fire wheel, buttercup, and goldenrod tell their own story. So do the pantaloon-shaped flowers of Dutchman's breeches. The red hearts of bleeding hearts. The ewer-shaped leaves of the pitcher plant. The skunk scent of skunk cabbage. The peppery seeds of peppergrass.

There are also a host of names that describe the medical properties, both real and imagined, that were attributed to certain plants—speedwell, feverfew, eye-balm, scurvy-grass, pleurisy root, colic-root, and the like. They need no translation either. Nor do the names that tell us where the plant is apt to grow, such as prairie fire, meadow rue, woodlily, bogberry, and stonecrop. And there are no hidden meanings behind the names that tell us what the plant does, so to speak. Lamb-kill, a small magenta-colored laurel, is indeed poisonous to young livestock. Sneezeweed supposedly makes us sneeze. Sticktight has burs that stick to our clothes and the coats of passing animals. Yellow rattle and rattlebox have seed pods that rattle when the pods are dry.

Another group of names that tell their own story are those given to native plants with a sidelong nod to the American Indian. There are close to a hundred of these—such nicknames as Indian blanket, Indian physic, Indian pipe, Indian tobacco, and moccasin flower. Unfortunately, the early explorers and colonists made little note of the Indian words for our rich variety of native flora. And the Indians had a name for every shrub and flower. Most of these, however, have been forgotten —disregarded and erased from memory over the years. A mere handful of Indian names survive in our botanic vocabulary, and some that we still use no longer have known translations. No one remembers the reason or the meaning for such Indian words as mesquite and yucca and cohosh and saguaro, the giant cactus of the southwest.

And somewhere along the line, down through the centuries, the original meanings of many Persian names were also lost and forgotten in the Old World; jasmine and alfalfa are two examples. The meanings of any number of Anglo-Saxon names are similarly lost; among them, thistle, clover, yarrow, and chicory which can no longer be explained.

What you will find in this dictionary is a roving collection

of plant names that *can* be translated—plant names that do not immediately explain themselves at first glance. Some have meanings hidden in Arabic, Sanskrit, Algonquian, ancient Germanic tongues, Greek, Latin, Spanish, and French. Some were drawn from mythology and from medieval legends. Other names were given in honor of early botanists. One of our wild plants is named for a French sea captain and explorer. Another for an early New York state politician. Another for the dove. Another for the beaver. Another for the bedbug. Here they are. The names behind the flower and plant names that we use without a second thought. Strawberry, mint, azalea, witch hazel, mistletoe, mustard, garlic, periwinkle, scuppernong, sagebrush. . . .
And the daisy. And the rose.

ADDER'S-TONGUE. See TROUT LILY

ANDROMEDA, a family of woody flowering plants, was named by Carolus Linnaeus, the Swedish naturalist (1707–1778), who dusted away medieval confusions and introduced our present-day scientific system of botany. And not a moment too soon. New trees and flowers from newly explored corners of the world were dumfounding European botanists. The plants found in America alone were undreamt of in their philosophies. How were they to classify phlox, pentstemons, magnolias, rhododendrons, bloodroot, wild bergamot, mountain laurel, trillium? The Linnaean system offered sure footing. Stated as simply as possible, Linnaeus classified plants by the number of stamens and pistils, and every species was assigned to a clan of related species. Andromeda became the name of a related group of woody plants, or heaths, whether members of the clan were found in Europe, Asia, or the New World.

There are several American heaths commonly known as andromeda, as well as having other local nicknames such as bog rosemary or moorwort; mountain andromedà or fetterbush (an unexplained name); and stagger-bush, said to afflict young sheep and cattle with "staggers," a cerebrospinal disorder.

Linnaeus' inspiration for the name andromeda came to him in a Lapland marsh in the summer of 1732. He was traveling alone, on horseback, on leave from the University of Uppsala. "I carried a small leather bag," he wrote. "This bag contained one shirt, two pairs of false sleeves and two half shirts; an inkstand, pencase, microscope and spying glass, a gauze cap to protect me occasionally from the gnats, a comb, my journal, and a parcel of paper stitched together for drying plants . . ." Later in his journal, Linnaeus made this entry:

> Scarcely any painter's art can so happily imitate the beauty of a fine female complexion; still less could any artificial colour upon the face itself bear a comparison with this lovely blossom. As I contemplated it I could not help thinking of Andromeda as described by the poets. . . . This plant is always fixed on some little turfy hillock in the midst of the swamps, as Andromeda herself was chained to a rock in the sea, which bathed her feet, as the fresh water does the roots of the plant. Dragons and venomous serpents surrounded her, as toads and other reptiles frequent the abode of her vegetable prototype, and, when they pair in the spring, throw mud and water over its leaves and branches. As the distressed virgin cast down her blushing face through excessive affliction, so does the rosy-coloured flower hang its head, growing paler and paler till it withers away. Hence, as this plant forms a new genus, I have chosen for it the name of Andromeda . . . —CAROLUS LINNAEUS, *Tour of Lapland* (*Lachesis Lapponica*), translated by James Smith, 1811

> *Staggerbush, or Andromeda.* No artist can do justice to its beauty as seen growing in favorable seasons in the rich, peaty, half-swampy barrens of New Jersey. Snow is white, but the whiteness of these flowers excels it.—THOMAS MEEHAN, *The Native Flowers and Ferns of the United States*, 1880

A N E M O N E—One of the first of the spring flowers, and, as Pliny tells it, a flower that can open only at the wind's bidding. Hence, their name from the Greek word for wind, *anemos*; and *anemos* can be traced back to Sanskrit—*aniti*, "he breathes," which is also the source word for animal and animation, to be breathing, to be alive.

According to one of the Greek myths, anemones sprang from the passionate tears shed by Venus over the body of the slain Adonis. In another myth, a nymph named Anemone was transformed into a frail spring flower by the goddess Flora, enraged with jealousy because Anemone was loved by Zephyr, the gentle

2

west wind. In keeping with these myths, there was an early connotation of sorrow and pain associated with anemones. In the Near East they were a symbol of illness, and according to an early European superstition, if you came to a field of anemones, you held your breath and ran past it, for the very wind that blew over the flowers was now poisoned.

Anemones grow around the world in the temperate zone. Some are poppy-like in the size of their flowers and the richness of their colors, others are pale and fragile in appearance, as are our native anemones, with the exception of the PASQUE-FLOWER.

The star anemone was used by the Tadoussacs of Quebec to brew a drink for any sickness. The root of Virginia anemone was used by the Menominees as a poultice for boils. The Meskwakis placed seeds of this plant on hot coals to produce smoke to revive unconscious persons. The Ojibways used "thimbleweed" root as a tea for lung congestion. The Canada anemone was used in a root tea as a wash for eye ailments. The same species was used by the Pillager Ojibwas as a throat lozenge, to clear the throat so they could sing well.—VIRGIL J. VOGEL, *American Indian Medicine,* 1970

They are never to be forgotten—that first bird pursued through thicket and over field with serious intent, not to kill but to know it, or that first plant lifted reverently and excitedly from the earth. No spring returns but that I wish I might live again through the moment when I went out in the woods and sat down with a book in my hands, to learn not only the name, but the ways and the range and the charm of the windflower, *Anemone quinquefolia.* —DONALD CULROSS PEATTIE, *An Alamanac for Moderns,* 1935

Brook Farm, May 1, 1841. My cold has almost entirely departed . . . but as the ground is so damp, and the atmosphere so chill, I intend to keep myself on the sick-list this one day longer, more especially as I wish to read Carlyle on Heroes . . . There has been but one flower found in this vicinity—and that was an anemone, a poor, pale, shivering little flower, that had crept under a stonewall for shelter.—NATHANIEL HAWTHORNE, to his fiancée, Miss Sophia Peabody

3

A R B U T U S is the ancient Latin name for the European strawberry tree, which has evergreen leaves, clusters of white and pink flowers, and a strawberry-like fruit that Pliny described as being so sour, one berry was enough. Trailing arbutus, native to the northeastern states and Canada, was named for the European strawberry tree, though no one seems to know just why. Presumably because of its evergreen leaves and the pinkish-white blossoms.

A symbol of approaching spring, a pet of poets and wildflower fanciers, trailing arbutus has perhaps evoked more sentimental descriptions than any other New England flower. Tradition has it that these were the first flowers the Pilgrims found in bloom, and its common nickname, once upon a time, was mayflower, or "Plymouth Mayflower," as the hawkers used to cry when then they peddled arbutus on the city streets in early spring—particularly in the streets of Boston.

> Yet "God be praised!" the Pilgrim said,
>   Who saw the blossoms peer
> Above the brown leaves, dry and dead,
>   "Behold our Mayflower here!"
> —JOHN GREENLEAF WHITTIER, 1807–1892,
> *The Mayflowers*

Where in all the world's bouquet is there another such a darling of a flower? . . . Even now, along the lichen-dappled wall, I see the lingering strip of snow, gritty and speckled, and at its very edge, hiding beneath the covering leaves, those modest little faces looking out at me. . . . No other flower can breathe the perfume of the arbutus, that earthy, spicy fragrance, which seems as though distilled from the very leaf-mould at its root. Often on this sunny slope, so sheltered by dense pines and hemlocks, have these charming clusters, pink and white, burst into bloom beneath the snow in March; and even on a certain late February day, we discovered a little, solitary clump, fully spread, and fairly ruddy with the cold.—WILLIAM HAMILTON GIBSON, *Pastoral Days*, 1880

Those who know the flower only as it is sold in the city streets, tied with wet, dirty string into tight bunches, withered and forlorn, can have little idea of the joy of finding the pink, pearly blossoms freshly opened among the withered leaves of oak and chestnut, moss, and pine needles in which they nestle close to the cold earth in the leafless, windy northern forest. . . . There is little use trying to coax this shyest of sylvan flower into our gardens where other members of its family, rhododendrons, laurels, and azaleas make themselves delightfully at home. It is wild as a hawk, an untamable creature that pines to death when brought into contact with civilization. Greedy street venders, who ruthlessly tear up the plant by the yard, and others without even the excuse of eking out a paltry income by its sale, have already exterminated it within a wide radius of our Eastern cities.—NELTJE BLANCHAN, *Nature's Garden*, 1901

A R E T H U S A, beautiful and bizarre, a wild orchid with only two known varieties. One grows in Japan, the other in North America. In Bulfinch's *Mythology*, the nymph Arethusa tells her own story: "One day I was returning from the wood . . . when I came to a stream silently flowing. . . . I stepped in knee deep, and not content with that, I laid my garments on the willows and I went in. While I sported in the water, I heard an indistinct murmur . . . and made haste to escape. The voice said, 'Why do you fly, Arethusa? I am Alpheus, the god of this stream.' I ran, he pursued. . . . At last, exhausted, I cried for help to Diana."

Diana heard the cry for help and in one of the innumerable metamorphoses that so delighted the Greek gods and goddesses, she transformed the pursued nymph into a fountain. Arethusa's name was chosen by a Dutch botanist, Dr. Johann Friedrich Gronovius (1690–1760) to whom newly discovered American plants were often sent for his study and classification. Just as Linnaeus romanticized over Andromeda, Dr. Gronovious imagined the American orchid to be a maiden in the midst of a spring that bubbled from bogs and marshes, where no one, presumably, could follow or find her.

Concord, Massachusetts. June 23, 1843. There ought to be a record of the procession of wild-flowers. . . . Above all, the noting

5

ARETHUSA

of the appearance of the first roses should not be omitted; nor of the Arethusa, one of the delicatest, gracefullest, and in every manner sweetest, of the whole race of flowers. For a fortnight past I have found it in the swampy meadows, growing up to its chin in heaps of wet moss. Its hue is a delicate pink, of various depths of shade, and somewhat in the form of a Grecian helmet. To describe it is a feat beyond my powers.—NATHANIEL HAWTHORNE, 1804–1864, *American Note-Books*

One flower to a plant, and that one rarely maturing seed; a temptingly beautiful prize which few refrain from carrying home, to have it wither on the way; pursued by a more persistent lover than Alpheus, the orchid-hunter who exports the bulbs to European collectors—little wonder this exquisite orchid is rare, and that from certain of those cranberry bogs of Eastern New England, which it formerly brightened with its vivid pink, it has now gone forever . . . —NELTJE BLANCHAN, *Nature's Garden*, 1901

ARTEMISIA—This is a worldwide genus of aromatic plants, usually with silver-gray foliage and inconspicuous flowerheads. Though artemesia is their botanic name, it's often used as a common name—an easy identification for such varieties as SAGEBRUSH, dusty miller, southernwood, old man, wormwood, and mugwort.

Some authorities say it commemorates Queen Artemisia of ancient history, who supposedly discovered the medical virtues of

6

this genus and gave them her own name to show that they were *her* royal herbs. Others say, with equal authority, that the genus was dedicated to Artemis, the Greek goddess of the moon and the hunt, who also protected mortals from pestilence and disease. But whoever their patroness, native artemisias have been used in medicine by the Chinese, the Europeans, and the American Indians for worms, gout, baldness, tonics, and poultices.

Wormwood and mugwort are old English nicknames for the artemisias, sometimes referring to the entire genus, sometimes to a specific plant, such as common mugwort, western mugwort, tall wormwood, annual wormwood, and absinthe wormwood. (There's no end to the mish-mash of names here.) For starters, wormwood —a fascinating-looking word—has little or no etymological history. It's the English version of the German *Wermut*, from the Old High German *Werimuota*. Wermut is wormwood and wormwood is *wermut*. Whatever original meaning it may have had is lost in the past. But this is where we get the word vermouth, the French version of *wermut*, because certain white wines were flavored with herbs such as wormwood.

As for absinthe wormwood, or *Artemisia absinthium,* the prime ingredient in a bitter and toxic french liqueur, its original Greek name was *apsinthion*, which also has no known translation. Absinthe, imported from Europe for American herb gardens, now grows wild throughout southern Canada and the northern United States.

To get back to mugwort, I've run across charming nonsense that explains the name as a throwback to its use in polishing and scouring pewter mugs. Quite simply, it comes from the Anglo-Saxon *Mucgwyrt*. A *mucg* was a midge or a gnat, and the scent of the plant's leaves repelled all such insect pests, including ants in the pantry.

On the Missouri River. Went early to the bluffs, to the south-westward, on one of which I observed fourteen buffaloe skulls placed in a row. The cavities of the eyes and the nostrils were filled with a species of *Artemisia* common on the prairies . . . On

7

my return, I caused our interpreter to enquire into the reason for this, and found that it was an honour conferred on the buffaloes which the Indians had killed, in order to appease their spirits, and prevent them from apprising the living buffaloes of the danger they run in approaching the neighborhood.—JOHN BRADBURY, *Travels in the Interior of America*, 1809–1811

The sand bar of Eastham is the sea wall of the inlet. . . . In four or five places storms have washed gullies or "cuts" clean through the wall. Dune plants grow in these dry beds, rooting themselves in under old, half-buried wreckage, clumps of dusty miller, *Artemisia stelleriana*, being the most familiar. The plant flourishes in the most exposed situations, it jumps from the dune rim to the naked slopes, it even tries to find a permanent station on the beach. Silvery gray-green all summer long, in autumn it puts on gold and russet-golden colourings of singular delicacy and beauty.—HENRY BESTON, *The Outermost House*, 1928

A R U M—The Arabians had the first word for it, *ar*, or fire, because of the fiery flavor of the roots. Among the wild arums native to America, there is skunk cabbage, jack-in-the-pulpit, dragon arum (or green dragon), water arum (or wild CALLA), and arrow arum.

The arrow arum, a large handsome arrow-leafed plant, is also known as tuckahoe, one of the few words of Indian origin to have survived the white man's botanizing. In the Algonquian tongue, this meant a bulbous plant used for food. John Eliot, the "Apostle to the Indians," who settled in Massachusetts in 1631, also defined tuckahoe as a round loaf or a cake of bread—a logical extension of the word, since flour from the tuckahoe root was used in baking.

The pronunciation varied from place to place along the Eastern seaboard. Captain John Smith, in the South, wrote it down as *tockawhoughe*. In the North, it was recorded as *taw-ho* and *tuckah*. Scholars, meanwhile, listed it as *Arum virginica*.

The chief root they have for food they called *tockawhoughe*.

ARROW ARUM OR TUCKAHOE

It groweth like a flag in marshes. In one day a savage will gather sufficient for a week. They cover a great many of them with oak leaves and fern, and then cover all with earth in the manner of a coal-pit; over it on each side they continue a great fire twenty-four hours before they dare eat it. Raw it is no better than poison, and being roasted, mixed with sorrel or meal and such like, it will prickle and torment the throat extremely, and yet in summer they use this ordinarily for bread.—CAPTAIN JOHN SMITH, *The General History of Virginia*, 1624

It is remarkable that the arums, with the plants next akin to them, are eaten by men in different parts of the world, though their roots, when raw, are almost poisonous. How can men have learned that plants so extremely opposite to our nature were eatable, and that their poison, which burns on the tongue, can be conquered by fire? Thus the root, which grows in the north of Europe, is sometimes used instead of bread in an emergency. The North American Indians eat arum. Those of South America, and of the West Indies eat other species of arums. The Hottentots at the Cape of Good Hope in Africa, prepare bread from a species of arum, which is as burning and poisonous as the other species of this plant. In the same manner, they employ the roots of some kinds of arum as a food, in Egypt and Asia. Probably, that severe but sometimes useful teacher, necessity, has first taught men to find out a food, which the first taste would have rejected as useless. —PETER KALM, *Travels into North America*, 1748–1751

Jack-in-the-pulpit—The roots have been much used by the American Indians as a bread flour. They are intensely acrid when fresh and can cause blisters, so don't even *think* of eating them raw. They have to be dried for at least 6 months. They can then be peeled, cut into small pieces, roasted in the oven for at least an hour and ground in a flour or coffee grinder until quite fine. The flavor is pleasant, almost chocolatey; but I'm not sure that I found it worth all the trouble. . . . The roots of Skunk Cabbage can be prepared in the same manner.—ADRIENNE CROWHURST, *The Weed Cookbook,* 1972

A S T E R is the Greek word for star, an apt name for a flower with a yellow center and multi-petaled rays; starwort is an old nickname that was used in early herbals and flower books, with aster listed as a secondary name. *Aster,* of course, is the source for a host of other star-fraught words—astronaut, astrology, astronomy, asterisk (the "little star"), and disaster (to be "ill-starred").

These flowers range around the world in hundreds of varieties —white, pink, blue, purple. Pliny recommended a brew of asters for snake-bite and an amulet of asters as a panacea for sciatica. Virgil prescribed the root of aster as a physic for sickly bees. The Shakers used a concoction of asters to clear up skin disorders.

In New England on the slow roll of October hills, I have seen purple asters toss out sprangles of flowers dyed in the fresh squeezed juices of the grape. And in Kansas along hedge roads where wagons climb wearily a little hill, there have I gathered these flowers of Paradise. They are stars fetched from the night skies and planted on the fields of day.—WILLIAM A. QUAYLE, *God's Calendar,* 1907

In the Garden of Marshall de Biron, at Paris, consisting of fourteen acres, every walk is button-holed on each side by lines of flower-pots, which succeed in their season. When I saw it there were nine thousand pots of asters.—HORACE WALPOLE, 1717–1797

Europe has no asters at which an American would look twice.

10

In this our western world the asters stand all through autumn, shoulder to shoulder in forest, on prairie, from the Atlantic to California, climbing up to the snows of Shasta, creeping out upon the salt marshes of Delaware. Here some call the white ones frostflower, for they come as the frost comes, as a breath upon the landscape, a silver rime of chill flowering in the old age of the year. In the southern mountains they are hailed as "farewell-summer." Farewell to August, to burning days. Farewell to corn weather. Farewell to swallows . . . —DONALD CULROSS PEATTIE, *An Almanac for Moderns*, 1935

A T A M A S C O   L I L Y—the lily that is not a lily, but a member of the amaryllis family. No matter. It is purely lilylike in its appearance, a large white waxy flower that points upward, and its other common names are fairy lily, swamp lily, and zephyr lily—the last given because it blooms when the spring zephyrs blow.

Atamasco is another of the few Indian names for our native plants that were listened to, written down, and remembered. This was a Virginian Indian word, *attamusco,* meaning "it is stained with red," which presumably refers to the reddish-pink color of the buds and the root stalks. The roots, like so many of our bulbous plants, were used by the Indians for food, though the leaves

ATAMASCO LILY

were known to be poisonous to livestock. Stagger-grass is another local nickname, because young stock feeding on the leaves are stricken with the "staggers"—a cerebrospinal disease also caused by one of our native andromeda. But as a New World beauty for the garden, atamasco lilies became immediately popular. Thomas Jefferson, for example, ordered selected bulbs from a Philadelphia nurseryman and planted them at Monticello in 1812.

A one-flowered lily, held in like esteem, in Virginia and North Carolina, as the daisy in England. It grows from a bulb that resembles an Onion minus the latter's customary odor, and gives great beauty to southern fields and forests.—JOHN RUSSELL BART-LETT, *Dictionary of Americanisms*, 1877

A Z A L E A is a Latin word meaning the "dry plant," from the Greek *azaleos,* to be dry or parched. The name was given by Linnaeus in the belief that azaleas thrive only in dry soil. Over 700 varieties have been discovered to date, the richest source being the fastnessess of southwestern China. Add to these the list of hybrids created over the years, and like the ancient theological riddle—How many angels can stand on the head of a pin?—you have an unaccountable number of azaleas.

FLAME AZALEA

They were introduced to the western world by the Dutch East India Company, in the 1600's, with a shipment of Japanese plants. From America, early in the 1700's, came the flame azalea, the swamp azalea, and the pink azalea or Pinxterbloom. Pinxter, by the way, has nothing to do with the color of the flowers. It's a Dutch word for Whitsuntide, the name given by Dutch settlers in honor of the season in which these azaleas bloomed. Peter Kalm, the Swedish botanist who visited America in the 1750's, wrote: "The people have not yet found that this plant may be applied to any practical use; they only gather the flowers and put them in pots, because they are so beautiful."

In 1835, so the story goes, a Belgian baker who was an enthusiastic off-hours horticulturist crossed the American breeds with the Pontic azalea from Asia Minor and created one of the most popular of the hybrids, the Ghent azalea, which became the national flower of Flanders.

At the confluence of the Broad and Savanna Rivers, May, 1778:
How harmonious and sweetly murmur the purling rills and fleeting brooks, roving along the shadowy vales, passing through dark, subterranean caverns, or dashing over steep rocky precipes, their cold, humid banks condensing the volatile vapours, which falling coalesce in crystalline drops, on the leaves and elastic twigs of the aromatic shrubs and incarnate flowers! In these cool, sequestered, rocky vales, we behold the fiery Azalea, flaming on the ascending hills or wavy surface of the gliding brooks. The epithet fiery, I annex to this most celebrated species of Azalea, as being expressive of the appearance of its flowers, which are in general of the colour of the finest red lead, orange and bright gold, as well as yellow and cream colour; these various splendid colours are not only in separate plants but frequently all the varieties and shades are seen in separate branches on the same plant; and the clusters of the blossoms cover the shrubs in such incredible profusion of the hill sides, that suddenly opening to view from dark shade, we are alarmed with the apprehension of the hill being set on fire.
—WILLIAM BARTRAM, *Travels,* 1773–1778

June 5, 1869—Azalea occidentalis, another charming shrub,

grows beside cool streams hereabouts and much higher in the Yosemite region. We found it this evening in bloom a few miles above Greeley's Mill, where we camped for the night. It is closely related to the rhododendrons, is very showy and fragrant, and everybody must like it not only for itself but for the shady alders and willows, ferny meadows, and living water associated with it. . . .

June 7—The sheep were sick last night, and many of them are still far from well, hardly able to leave camp, coughing, groaning, looking wretched and pitiful, all from eating the leaves of the blessed azalea. So at least say the shepherd and the Don. Having had but little grass since they left the plains, they are starving, and so eat anything green they can get. Sheep men call azalea "sheep-poison," and wonder what the Creator was thinking about when he made it . . . —JOHN MUIR, *My First Summer in the Sierra,* 1911

B

BACHELOR'S BUTTONS. See under KNAP-WEED

B A N E—henbane, dogbane, baneberry, cowbane, fleabane, wolfsbane, bugbane. This is a word with dark, dire connotations. It comes from *bana,* the Anglo-Saxon word for a murderer or destroyer, and it was used for those plants and wildflowers that were poisonous or at least repellent to the animals named. Some, like henbane, cowbane, and wolfsbane, are poisonous to humans as well.

As far as I know, there are no plants in North America that will lay you out stone cold dead in two seconds. There are, however, plants which . . . can do nasty things to stomach and head. It is important that one is aware of them. *Baneberry*—The attractive and decorative clusters of berries may be very interesting to

14

RED BANEBERRY

children. They should be taught to leave them well alone for they have been known to cause heavy dizziness. *Dogbane*—The young shoots of the Dogbanes may well be confused with those of Milkweed, so beware. They are extremely cathartic and are known to have poisoned young cattle. *Henbane*—Though the flowers are quite attractive, the rest of the plant, with its slimy hairs and foul smell, is hardly likely to attract the forager, though children should certainly be warned against it. Henbane is the possessor of the strongly hypnotic poison, *hyoscyanin*, and should certainly not be messed with.—ADRIENNE CROWHURST, *The Weed Cookbook*, 1972

The force of the Wolfes-banes is most pernicious and poisonsome . . . to which purpose it is brought into Mart-townes to be sold unto hunters, the juice therof being prepared by pressing forth, when they mean to infect their arrowheads, the more speedily and deadly to dispatch the wild beasts.—JOHN GERARD, *Herbal*, 1597

Fleabane—We all know the fleabanes, or little daisies, that spring up in the meadows and along the roadsides in summer. . . . Country people tell us that when burned they are obnoxious to insect life, and we frequently see dried bunches of them hanging over their cottage doors to caution such intruders against entering the portal.

15

Cowbane, or *Water Hemlock—*It is unfortunate that so many common names have been bestowed upon this unworthy plant, which is known as spotted cowbane, beaver poison, sneezeweed, and children's bane. They serve rather to prevent its becoming generally recognized as the deadly water hemlock. Its appearance also is such that it is frequently mistaken for the wild carrot and sweet cicely. . . . Of all members of the parsley family it is the most poisonous.—ALICE LOUNSBERRY, *A Guide to the Wildflowers,* 1899

In shaded hollows and on the hill-sides, the tall white wands of the black cohosh [origin unknown], or bugbane, shoot upward, rocket-like. The great stout stems, large divided leaves and slender spikes of the feathery flowers render this the most conspicuous wood-plant of the season. If we chance to be lingering when the last sunlight has died away, and happen suddenly upon one of these ghostly groups, the effect is almost startling. The rank odor of the flowers detracts somewhat from one's enjoyment of their beauty, and is responsible for their unpleasing title of bugbane. —FRANCES THEODORA PARSONS, *According to the Seasons,* 1902

BASKET-FLOWER. See under KNAPWEED

BEADLILY. See CLINTONIA

BEARD-TONGUE. See PENTSTEMON

BEE-BALM. See BERGAMOT

BENJAMIN BUSH, or spicebush, blooms in March and early April in damp, shaded places. The name Benjamin is an early English variation on benzoin—a "corruption" of benzoin, as etymologists would phrase it. In the Old World, benzoin was an aromatic resin used in ointments, incense, and perfume and came from benzoin trees native to southeastern Asia. The original word was Arabic, *luban jawi,* which meant "frankincense of Java." In Italian, it was adapted as *lo-benzoi,* and from there, became benzoin. Because the spicy scent of the American shrub was reminiscent of "Javanese frankincense," benzoin or Benjamin bush became its name. Dried and powdered berries were used as a substitute for imported allspice during the Revolutionary War and the leaves as a substitute for tea. An Asiatic species is used for making toothpicks because of its aromatic fragrance.

Even before the scaly catkins on the alders become yellow, or the silvery velvet pussy willows expand to welcome the earliest bees that fly, this leafless bush breathes a faint spicy fragrance in the bleak gray woods. Its only rivals among the shrubbery, the service-berry and its twin sister the shad-bush, have scarcely had the temerity to burst into bloom when the little clusters of lemon-yellow flowers, cuddled close to the naked branches, give us our first delightful spring surprise. . . . —NELTJE BLANCHAN, *Nature's Garden,* 1901

When maple sap has been reduced about 4 to 1 by boiling, it has about the right sweetness for making some interesting woodland teas. A cupful of chopped-up bark of the fragrant spicebush boiled for twenty minutes in 1 quart of this sweet sap will give a palatable tea that formerly had a reputation as a restorative and reliever of fatigue. Whether the tiredness of the early settlers was relieved by the sugar, warmth and rest they acquired while making and drinking this tea, or whether the spice bush actually contains some stimulant is for a more scientific researcher than I am to decide. Its pleasant flavor and invigorating effect are all the excuses I need to drink Spicebush Tea.—EUELL GIBBONS, *Stalking the Wild Asparagus,* 1962

B E R G A M O T—American flowers of the mint family, which come in three delicious colors—bright red, pale lilac, and purple. They were first described in a sixteenth century Spanish treatise on New World botany, and introduced to England in the 1630's by John Tradescent the younger (son of John Tradescent,

17

BERGAMOT

gardener to Charles I), who traveled in the Virginia area on a flower-hunting journey. The citrusy-minty scent was so reminiscent of the aromatic oil pressed from bergamot oranges (grown in and around Bergamo, Italy) that the common name for these handsome mints became wild bergamot.

Red bergamot was a particular favorite in English and European gardens, and there was the inevitable rash of nicknames for the scarlet flowers—Indian plume, fragrant balm, mountain mint, and the two we use so often today, bee balm or Oswego tea. Bee balm, of course, because the brilliant blossoms are always abuzz with bees, and, in American fields and gardens, ruby-throated hummingbirds and hummingbird moths seek out bee balm, too.

Oswego tea became a common name in the 1700's. John Bartram, the Quaker botanist from Philadelphia, traveled into northern New York state in 1743 with the two-man peace party sent to arrange a treaty between the Iroquois and Virginian nations. The trek took them to Fort Oswego, and among the plants Bartram gathered en route were an assortment of bergamots, which the Indians used in tea for chills or fevers. Thus, the new American nickname—Oswego tea. It is still recommended as a tea and found effective in cooling fevers. Further, a poultice of crushed leaves is soothing on insect bites. The Indians also used bergamot to cover up the bitterness of foul-tasting medicines and to scent their pomades made of bear grease, a cosmetic recipe they passed along to early settlers. As for John Bartram, his son William was also a naturalist and explorer and is quoted many times in these pages, under azalea, canna, iris, St. Johnswort, strawberry, and compass plant. The Bartram homestead, which John built with his own hands, still stands amid the gardens he laid out over two centuries ago. You will find him listed in the Philadelphia phone book under Bartram's Mansion and Gardens: 215/SA9-5281.

In the pasture, only a name now for this open piece of land beyond the walnut grove, the wild bergamot fills the air with its warm mint smell. It is lavender with no pretense of blue. We had red bergamot once . . . Bee balm, enormous, like Fourth of July explosions. A peculiar red, neither crimson nor luminous. A wood red.—JOSEPHINE W. JOHNSON, *The Inland Island*, 1969

We have so few red flowers that when one flashes suddenly upon us it gives us a pleasant thrill of wonder and surprise. The red flowers know so well how to enhance their beauty by seeking an appropriate setting. They select the rich green backgrounds only found in a moist, shady place, and are peculiarly charming when associated with a lonely marsh or a mountain brook. The bee-balm especially haunts these cool nooks, and its rounded flower-clusters touch with warmth the shadows of the damp woods of midsummer. The Indians named the flower *O-gee-chee*—flaming flower.—MRS. WILLIAM STARR DANA, *How to Know the Wild Flowers*, 1893

B E T O N Y—According to Pliny, the European plant that first bore this name was originally known as vettonica, because the Vettones tribe of ancient Spain discovered its medical magic. Betony was believed to be a cure for almost every ill that flesh is heir to. What's more, it drove away evil spirits if planted in graveyards or worn in an amulet. So great indeed was its power, wrote Pliny, that snakes enclosed in a circle of betony lashed themselves to death. And the Romans had a proverb for it: "Sell your coat and buy betony."

This family of plants, with close to five hundred varieties, is found in the Arctic circle, Europe, the mountains of Asia, and across North America. All have fern-like leaves and tufts of helmet-like flowers. One of our western betonies is appropriately nicknamed red helmet, while others are descriptively known as elephant head and fern leaf and Indian warrior. The American wood-betony is also called beefsteak plant, because of the beefy-red turn of color in the blossoms. But wherever they grow, these plants are universally referred to in English as louseworts, with comparable louse-ridden nicknames in any number of European languages. (Thomas Meehan explains why in the following quotation.) Betonies, by the way, are difficult to transplant because of their symbiotic association with underground fungi that envelope the roots and supply the plant with nutrients absorbed from the soil.

> Common wood betony seeks shade from the warm sun by taking to open woods, or getting on rising knolls in swamps or low grounds where it may have the advantage of a humid atmosphere. The flowers are amongst the handsomest of our native plants, and the fern-like leaves set off to great advantage the floral beauty. The upper portion ranges from a light brown to a rich purple, while the lower portions are of a pure white, varying to a light yellow.
>
> In the northern countries of Europe the whole family is in bad odor with stock-raisers, from an idea that cattle, and sheep especially, feeding on them become lousy. Like many other old notions in agriculture, this is no doubt a libel on these beautiful flowering plants. But the impression induced Linneaus to give the name Pedicularis to this genus, meaning "to belong to a louse," and from it also comes the English name of Lousewort.—THOMAS MEEHAN, *The Native Flowers and Ferns of the United States*, 1880

We have seen in the snapdragon family how many of its members have curious expressive faces, resembling animals quite as much as often pansies take on the look of old men and women. The turtleheads are like tortoises; the monkey-flower tells its own story, and here, moreover, is the wood betony rearing its slender corolla as the head of a walrus and even with two miniature projections in imitations of his tusks. Most often the upper lip of the flower is purple and the under one pale red, but also they occur in yellow. . . . It is ever a strange-looking plant.—ALICE LOUNSBERRY, *A Guide to the Wild Flowers*, 1899

B L O O D R O O T, the wild, white, poppy of early spring, was named for the orange-red juice in its roots and stem that was used in the old days to cure coughs and colds and skin diseases— another bit of native medical lore passed onto the white man by the Indian. Indians also used the rootstocks as a dye for basket- ware and clothing and for painting their faces and bodies, which gave rise to another early name, Indian paint. Bloodroot was also known once upon a time as red puccoon, the name under which it is often listed in early wildflower books. Puccoon came from *pokan*, a Virginian Indian word for any red-juiced plant used for staining and dyeing, and *pokan* came from *pak*, meaning blood. (See POKEWEED.)

BLOODROOT

Many wild flowers which we have transplanted to our gardens are full of magic and charm. . . . In other flowers the quality of mystery is inherent. In childhood I absolutely abhorred Bloodroot; it seemed to me a fearsome thing when I first picked it. I remember well my dismay, it was so pure, so sleek, so innocent of face, yet bleeding at a touch, like a murdered man in the Blood Ordeal.—ALICE MORSE EARLE, *Old Time Gardens*, 1901

About the end of April, beside the road, on the brink of the river, in moist pastures, and beside the woodland brook, may be found the beautiful, broad white flowers of the plant which furnishes a famous specific for coughs and colds. Long before I became acquainted with the plant I had taken many drops of its orange-red blood on lump sugar.—F. SCHUYLER MATHEWS, *Familiar Flowers of Field and Garden*, 1895

Though the roots of the bloodroot have been candied and have been used extensively in medicine in the past, in large quantities they can produce vomiting, extreme dizziness and paralysis. Small doses are said to aid digestion and to be an effective remedy for coughs, colds and skin diseases. However, it is advisable to leave the Bloodroot well enough alone.—ADRIENNE CROWHURST, *The Weed Cookbook*, 1972

B O N E S E T is one of the towering wildflowers of late summer, often growing to five feet in height, with a broad head of dull white, downy flowers and distinctive leaves that join on either side of the stalk, as though the leaves were of one piece and the stalk had grown up through the middle. Boneset is a near relative to JOE-PYE WEED and a native American plant, whose medical virtues were recognized by the Indians and extolled by the whites for every ailment from "James River ringworm" to influenza. During the Civil War, when medical supplies were short, boneset tea was used by Confederate troops as a substitute for quinine in fighting fevers. The tea brewed from boneset leaves was most renowned as a cure for break-bone, or dengue, fever in the old South. Hence, the name boneset. Thoroughwort was another early name, because of its thoroughness in allaying fevers and agues of all kinds. As for the flavor of boneset tea, you'll see in the last three quotes given here that there was some sharp disagreement. I've never tasted it. I can add nothing to the controversy one way or the other.

Sure cure for bite of rattlesnake. The leaves of boneset herb boiled down in milk to a strong decoction, which is to be given freely as a drink; also keep the bitten part well poulticed with the same. A young woman living at Mahomeny Creek, Jefferson Co., Pa., was bitten by a snake in the morning. Her father rode 20 miles to Red Bank for a physician, but returning toward evening met a neighbor, Wm. Neil, who told him he knew how to cure her, and went home with him, proceeding on a run across the meadow, gathering some boneset as he went along. And, to save time, as he neared the house he chewed some of the leaves in his mouth to a pulp, and the moment he reached the girl, put the mass, as a poultice, on the wound. He then immediately made a milk decoction, as first explained, and gave a spoonful at a time, as she was able to take. At the time of his arrival, her tongue was so swollen as to protrude out of her mouth, and bleeding from the mouth and ears. He remained all night, frequently changing the boneset poultice. By morning she was able to close her mouth, and ceased bleeding at the nose and ears, and by evening was quite comfortable and was soon entirely restored.—D. MAGNER, *The New System,* 1883

To one whose childhood was passed in the country some fifty years ago the name or sight of this plant is fraught with unpleasant memories. The attic or wood-shed was hung with bunches of the dried herb, which served as so many grewsome warnings against wet feet, or any over-exposure which might result in cold or malaria. A certain Nemesis, in the shape of a nauseous draught, which was poured down the throat under the name of "boneset tea," attended such a catastrophe.—MRS. WILLIAM STARR DANA, *How to Know the Wild Flowers,* 1893

An old-fashioned illness known as break-bone fever once had

its terrors for a patient increased a hundredfold by the certainty he felt of taking nauseous doses of boneset tea, administered by zealous old women outside the "regular practice."—NELTJE BLANCHAN, *Nature's Garden*, 1901

Neltje Blanchan and Mrs. Dana call Thoroughwort or Boneset tea a "nauseous draught," and I thereby suspect that neither has tasted it: I have many a time, and it has a clear, clean bitter taste, no stronger than any bitter beer or ale . . . —ALICE MORSE EARLE, *Old Time Gardens*, 1901

B O U G A I N V I L L E A—The tropical American vine whose flower-bracts range, brilliantly, from crimson and deep purple to brick-red, pink, and bronzy-apricot. It was named for Louis Antoine de Bougainville who led the first French expedition around the world, a three-year voyage from 1766 to 1769. In those days, no explorer set sail without a naturalist, and Bougainville's choice was an elderly botanist, one Philibert de Commerson, who was accompanied by a young assistant of some twenty-seven years—Jean Baret. Baret, as described by Bougainville, was not particularly handsome, but quiet and hard-working, and at every stop he faithfully assisted the aged de Commerson, lugging the provisions, arms, and portfolios of plant specimens.

This dedicated assistant was, in truth, a young woman who had persuaded de Commerson to bring her along, in disguise as a man, because she wanted to sail around the world. And so she did. But in Tahiti their botanizing took a surprise turn. A young chief, far more observant than the crew of Bougainville's two ships, recognized the young man as a young woman, and one day while she and de Commerson were studying wildflowers along the shore, a hefty native carried her off, bodily. When Jean Baret was rescued, her dishevelled clothes revealed the facts of the matter to her amazed shipmates.

Bougainville accepted this switch-about with equanimity. From then on, she was known as Jeanne, not Jean, and continued on the voyage. Bougainville wrote, "I must do her the justice to acknowledge that at all times while she was on board ship she was the model of propriety. It must be admitted, however, that had the two vessels been shipwrecked in this vast ocean on some desert island Fate would have played some strange tricks on Baret." But fate had other plans for Jeanne Baret. She later married a soldier and though she disappeared without trace from the pages of history, it should be noted here that she was with Philibert de Commerson when they put ashore at Rio de Janeiro and there found the beautiful vine named in honor of Admiral Bougainville. It was cultivated as a garden plant in the United States, but took off on its own and now grows wild in our tropical and semitropical climates.

We walked in Mr. Ovey's gate—it was almost dark—stepped into his patio. The fountain was still, a few birds singing and thick sweet scents in the dark. What was it—the tuberose in the corner? The bougainvillea was a dark tangle against the sky, and the pine tree black beyond the roof. All the arches were lit, a lantern in each one. A man came around and lit small candles and set them in niches. A table was set under one arch and candles lit. We had supper there, looking out at the sky and the bougainvillea against it. . . . It was so perfect, so magical, so unreal—those small niches lighted, the lanterned arches, the cloudy moon half hid behind the bougainvillea . . . —ANNE MORROW LINDBERGH, *Bring Me a Unicorn*, 1972

B O U N C I N G B E T, or Soapwort. See under WORT

B U T T E R - A N D - E G G S. See TOADFLAX

B U T T E R F L Y T U L I P. See MARIPOSA

B U T T E R F L Y W E E D, or pleurisy-root, belongs to the milkweed family and is one of the showiest of our American wildflowers, with bright orange clusters that attract butterflies by the droves—monarchs, swallowtails, painted ladies, cabbage butterflies, sulphur butterflies, fritillaries, pearl crescents, tailed blues, coral hairstreaks.

The Indians used the orange blossoms as a dye, as well as for food, but its most important role was in Indian pharmacology. Hence this plant's early nickname of pleurisy-root, although it served as an internal and external remedy for many other ailments.

The pleurisy-root has received more attention as a medicine than any other species of this genus, having been regarded, almost since the discovery of this country, as a subtonic, diaphoretic, alterative, expectorant, diuretic, laxative, escharotic, carminative, anti-spasmodic, anti-pleuritic, stomachic, astringent, anti-rheumatic, anti-syphilitic, and what not.—DR. CHARLES MILLSPAUGH, *American Medicinal Plants*, 1887

Few if any of our native plants add more to the beauty of the midsummer landscape than . . . the gorgeous butterfly-weed, whose vivid flowers flame from dry sandy meadows with such luxuriance of growth as to seem almost tropical. Even in the tropics one hardly sees anything more brilliant than the great masses of color along some of our New England railways in July . . . The Indians used it as food and prepared a crude sugar from the flowers; the young seed-pods they boiled and ate with buffalo-meat. . . . Oddly enough, at the Centennial Exhibition Philadelphia, 1876 much attention was attracted by a bed of these beautiful plants which were brought from Holland. Truly, flowers, like prophets, are not without honor save in their own country. —MRS. WILLIAM STARR DANA, *How to Know the Wild Flowers*, 1893

It grows in dry sandy places, blooms in midsummer, and stains the pastures with a brilliant orange-color, which, I should think, would set a colorist of the impressionist school quite wild.—F. SCHUYLER MATTHEWS, *Familiar Flowers of Field and Garden*, 1895

26

CALICO BUSH. See LAUREL

CALLA, or water arum. The first time I saw wild callas was in a black-water bog in coastal Maine, where the rocks and fallen trees were overgrown with thick coats of emerald moss, and blooming throughout, up to the edge of a spruce forest, was a mat of white flowers. They were instantly recognizable. The calla is unique. (And they were savagely guarded by swarms of starving mosquitoes.)

Calla is believed to come from the Greek *kalos*, meaning beautiful. The wild callas of North American bogs are the same species as the callas that are abundant in European bogs through Holland, Germany, Scandinavia, Russia, and Siberia. The Indians ground the roots into flour, as they did with other native arums, and they were used in the same manner throughout Europe.

The single white petal that makes the calla so distinctive is not a petal at all. It's the bract, which in most flowers is the green leaf-like underpinning that holds the blossom. The true flowers of the calla are massed on the club, or spadix, that is sheltered by the white bract. Cultivated callas are a South African plant. Though the name is the same, the two callas are not classified in t..e same genus, because of highly technical differences in the structure of their anthers and the cell division of the ovaries.

Yes, it is done. The winter is over and past, and "The time of the singing birds is come." They are at it beak and claw,—the red-birds, and the cat-birds, and the chattering jays, and the twittering sparrows, busy and funny and bright. Down in the swamp-land fronting our cottage, four calla-lily buds are just unfolding themselves.—HARRIET BEECHER STOWE, *Palmetto-Leaves*, 1873

This little plant wafts across the mind visions of an underworld garden. And if there is such a place the flowers there must surely glance upward and think of the wild callas as fairies that have flown above; for much mystery lies in their dainty whiteness. They have luxurious relatives living in greenhouses, and although the cultivated calla has snobbishly disowned this dweller of the ditches and watery place, the family resemblance is very striking. —Alice Lounsberry, *A Guide to the Wild Flowers*, 1899

C A L O P O G O N, or grass-pink, is another of the exquisite North American orchids. The name means "beautiful beard," from the Greek *kalos*, beautiful, and *pogon*, beard. In July, 1852, Thoreau mused over the calopogon blooming in the grass at the edge of a blueberry swamp and wrote in his journal that the pink-purple orchids were perfect flowers—fair, delicate, and nymph-like —and that they deserved a more becoming name. Perhaps, he decided, the name of one of the Naiades. But calopogon it is, though the bright yellow "beard" is not on the lower petal, as in other orchids, but on the top petal, like a topknot.

I remember well the first time I ever the Calopogon at home. It was one morning late in June, while taking a walk with a friend and her little girl. We had just crossed a wet meadow, bright with the fronds of ferns, the rank foliage of the false hellebore, and the canary-yellow of the day-blooming evening primrose.

28

As we reached the comparatively firm ground which skirted the woods, our eyes fell upon a patch of feathery grasses and radiant Calopogons.

Knowing only too well the childish instinct immediately to rush upon such a mass of floral loveliness, my first thought was to shield with outstretched arms the delicate beauties, hesitating to pick even a single blossom until we had feasted our eyes upon their unruffled grace. After all, how much better it is to retain a memory of some enchanted spot unrifled of its charm, than to bear away a burden of blossoms, which nearly always seem to leave half their beauty behind them.—Mrs. WILLIAM STARK DANA, *How to Know the Wild Flowers*, 1893

C A L T R O P. See KNAPWEED

C A L Y P S O, a North American orchid sometimes known as fairy-slipper, wears a cock's comb of pink petals over a yellow, white, and pink slipper-like lower petal.

It was Calypso, a sea nymph and the goddess of silence, who detained Ulysses on her island for seven years with promises of immortality if he would stay forever. Her name in Greek means "she who conceals," from *kaluptein*, to cover or conceal. Because this elusive flower grows in hidden places, Calypso's name was selected late in the 1700's by R. A. Salisbury, an English botanist, who evidently was influenced by Linnaeus' earlier flower names borrowed from nymphs and Greek maidens.

Even when her sanctuary is discovered Calypso does not always reveal herself. The ground and the fallen tree-trunks are thickly padded with moss and embroidered with trailing vines of snow-berry and twin-leaf; painted trilliums dot with their white stars the shadows lying under the tangled fragrant branches, the silence of the forest, disturbed only by the chirr of a squirrel or the sudden jubilance of the oven-bird, envelops you and seems the proper accompaniment of such an expedition. You follow, perhaps, a winding path made by the wild animals among the underbrush, moving slowly, and you easily overlook the dainty blossom, nestling

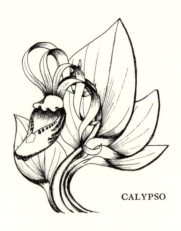

CALYPSO

in some soft, damp nook, and poised lightly on its stem as if ready to flutter away between your covetous fingers.—HENRY BALDWIN, *Orchids of New England*, 1884

Calypso is a May orchid which I have not yet found growing in this part of the world (southern New York State). But early one June I had the good luck to see it flowering on the lower slopes of the Canadian Rockies, though unfortunately the majority of the blossoms had been plucked from the plants in order to decorate the tables of the hotel dining-room at Banff . . . —FRANCES THEODORA PARSONS, *According to the Seasons*, 1902

C A M A S S, or Quamash—one of the loveliest of the native American wildflowers—is a western species that was used by the Indians for food. The word camass comes from the Chinook language and means, simply, "a bulb." Among the Nootka Indians of British Columbia, a similar word—*chamas*—meant "pleasant to the taste." Its English nickname is wild hyacinth.

September 20, 1805. A man came out to meet the party, with great caution, but he conducted them to a large tent in the village, and all the inhabitants gathered round to view with a mixture of fear and pleasure these wondrous strangers. The conductor now informed Captain Clark by signs, that the spacious tent was the residence of the great chief, who had set out three days ago with

30

all the warriors to attack some of their enemies towards the south-west . . . and that in the meantime there were only a few men left to guard the women and children. They now set before them a small piece of buffaloe meat, some dried salmon, berries, and several kinds of roots. Among these last is one which is round and much like an onion in appearance and sweet to the taste: it is called quamash, and is eaten either in its natural state, or boiled into a kind of soup or made into a cake. After the long abstinence this was a sumptuous treat; we returned the kindness of the people by a few small presents, and then went on.—MERIWETHER LEWIS, *The Lewis and Clark Expedition*, 1804–1806

Cammas. A new species of plant found in the valley of the Columbia river. It has a truncated root in the form of an onion, and grows in moist rich land. It is prepared for eating by first roasting, then pounding, after which it is made into loaves like bread. It has a liquorice taste . . . —CUTHBERT W. JOHNSON, ESQ., *Farmer's Encyclopaedia*, 1852

In some localities these plants are found covering meadows and marshy tracts in great profusion. They bear beautiful clusters of showy-blue flowers, somewhat like the hyacinth in habit, and have long been favorites in European gardens.

Grizzly bears, when more plentiful in the early days, were particularly fond of the bulbs; and the northern Indians today value them very highly as an article of diet . . . Indeed, the Nez Percé Indian war in Idaho [1877] was caused by encroachments upon the territory which was especially rich in these bulbs. . . . There is a white-flowered form of this same species, whose bulb is said to be poisonous.—MARY ELIZABETH PARSONS, *Wild Flowers of California*, 1900

CAMOMILE, or CHAMOMILE is another runaway now listed as a wildflower. An ancient medicinal herb, it was brought from Europe for colonial gardens. The Egyptians used the flowers in ointments, the Romans used them internally for liver complaints, the Saxons used them for eye diseases, the Elizabethans planted it in grassy walks so that the sweet smell

CAMOMILE

would rise under your feet as you wandered down the garden path, and camomile is still brewed into a fragrant, pale gold tea that soothes the nerves, calms hysterics, and relieves fevers and colic. It was this fragrance that gave the plant its name, earth-apple, from the Greek *chamai*, on the ground or earth, and *melon*, apple. Chamai, by the way, is the root word for chameleon—the "ground lion."

Another variety is known as mayweed, or stinking camomile (with a taste to match), and also is used in tranquilizing tisanes or teas. But I have never drunk a cup of it, so perhaps the matter of taste is purely personal, like the old controversy over the flavor of boneset tea. Camomile teas are still popularly used as rinses to give one's hair a reddish tint.

"Now I'm goin' right down to get us each a mug o' my beer," she announced as we entered the house, "An' I believe I'll sneak in a little mite o' camomile. Goin' to a funeral an' all, I feel to have had a very wearin' afternoon." I heard her going down into the cool little cellar, and then there was considerable delay. When she returned, mug in hand, I noticed the taste of camomile, in spite of my protest, but its flavor was disguised by some other herb that I did not know, and she stood over me until I drank it all and said that I liked it.—SARAH ORNE JEWETT, *The Country of the Pointed Firs*, 1896

C A M P I O N—This is a large and confusing group of flowers. There are the cultivated varieties, there are the wild campions from Europe now growing wild in America from coast to coast, and there are our *native* wild campions. To top it off, many of the campions are also known as catchflies, and all of them are members of the pink family—therefore you also have campions, or catchflies that go by such names as mullein pink, fire pink, and wild pink.

Even in the definition of campion there is confusion. The name obviously comes from the Latin *campus*, or field, but authorities disagree as to whether campion means "field flower," or whether it comes from *campione*, a battlefield, from having been woven into chaplets with which champions in the public games were crowned. But there is no problem with "catchfly." That name was given because many flowers of this family exude a sticky substance in which crawling insects are apt to get mired down.

The nightflowering catchfly opens only toward evening, or on cloudy days. It blooms side by side with the evening primrose, and might easily be taken for a white variety of the latter flower by one who consults his imagination rather than his botany. This catchfly is the most beautiful thing imaginable under the magnifying glass; the petals are not so remarkable, but the calyx (the protecting green envelope of the flower) is as delicate as though it were modeled in spun glass; the translucent line of green and white, the symmetry of the tiny form, are all worth the closest examination. If the plant had been formed of the most fragile and delicately colored glass it could scarcely have been more curious or beautiful.—F. Schuyler Mathews, *Familiar Flowers of Field and Garden*, 1895

If you ask any farmer in the Middle Eastern States and westward through the Prairies for his opinion of Bladder Campion, he will probably tell you it is a gol-danged weed—or stronger words to that effect. From his standpoint he is quite correct, for this self-assertive plant from Europe, North Africa and Asia is extremely difficult to eradicate from pastures and hayfields once it gains a foothold in them. Yet there can be no denial of the astounding effect of the plant's peculiar bulbous blossoms or their effectiveness as they sway in the wind and sunlight of the wide open spaces. Bladder campion has a variety of common names, including Bladder Catchfly, Cowbell and White Ben.—ROBERT S. LEMMON, *Wildflowers of North America*, 1961

The rosy finch was there, hopping about in the snow, and the pipit soared and sang in the warm, lucid air above us. Below it a white ptarmigan rose up and wheeled about, uttering a curious hoarse croaking sound, and dropped back to his mate on the rocks. In keeping with these delicate signs of bird life were the little pink flowers, a species of moss campion, blooming here and there just below the snow-line.—JOHN BURROUGHS, *In Green Alaska*, 1901

C A N N A is a Latin word meaning a reed, and the name was given because of the plants' tall, reed-like stalks. Cannas are native to the tropics (Central and South America, Malaysia, Nepal), with two species indigenous to our southern states. Because the hard, round, shiny seeds resemble bullets, the American nickname for canna is Indian shot. In South America, the Indians put the seeds in nutshells, strung them like a necklace, and used them as rattles. Early in the sixteenth century, Spanish missionaries sent these rattle seeds back to Spain—not to be planted for their flowers, but to be used as rosary beads.

Louisiana. August, 1777. Fire and smoke were insufficient to expel the hosts of mosquitoes that invested our camp, and kept us awake during the long and tedious night, so that the alligators had no chance of taking us napping. We were glad to rise early in the morning, proceeding up the Amite. . . . The trees are of an incredible magnitude. The Canna Indica grows here in surprising luxuriance, presenting a glorious show; the stem rises six, seven and nine feet high, terminating upwards with spikes of scarlet flowers.—WILLIAM BARTRAM, *Travels*, 1773–1777

Let a flower suffer the sneers of the gardening cognescenti, and all the fine hybrids of it that some faithful soul may create will flourish to little advantage. Cannas are a case in point. Mention them, and across the mind flashes unlovely memories of park, prison, and hospital garden beds. For years the Canna was an institutional flower, and that's enough to damn any plant. Yet some very beautiful hybrids have been created and at the sight of them we were ecstatic over the subtle pinks and yellows. Had they ceased being institutional? We tried them first in the cutting garden to see if they were so terrible as we had feared and then, finding them really beautiful, gave them a place in the borders.

—RICHARDSON WRIGHT, *The Gardener's Bed-Book*, 1939

CARDINAL FLOWER—The reddest of reds, cardinal red, the brilliant color worn by the cardinals of the Roman Church. It's an eye-popping red when you suddenly come upon it around the bend of a river on an August day and find cardinal flowers ablaze along the shore.

In its original meaning, cardinal comes from the Latin *cardo*, or hinge, and the title was given to ecclesiastical dignitaries in the fifth century, because the administration of the church "hinged" on the college of cardinals. The choice of cardinal as a name for the plant was given in France, perhaps with Cardinal Richelieu in mind. He was in his hey-day as a power at the French court when the first cardinal flowers were sent home by French missionaries in North America. By 1629, the name was in common usage on the continent, when John Parkinson, the English botanist, wrote that he had received a shipment of seeds from Paris: "The rich crimson cardinal flower . . . it groweth neere the river of Canada, where the French plantation in America is seated." As a garden plant, the cardinal flower was an instant success in Europe. When the Empress Josephine had her nursery of exotica at Malmaison, cardinal flowers grew there among the rare and beautiful from all known corners of the world. It is a member of the LOBELIA family, and was used as a worm medicine by the American Indians.

Concord, Massachusetts. August 13, 1842. For the last two or

three days, I have seen scattered stalks of the cardinal-flower, the gorgeous scarlet of which it is a joy even to remember. The world is made brighter and sunnier by flowers of such a hue. Even perfume, which otherwise is the soul and spirit of a flower, may be spared when it arrays itself in this scarlet glory. It is a flower of thought and feeling, too; it seems to have its roots deep down in the hearts of those who gaze at it. Other bright flowers sometimes impress me as wanting sentiment; but it is not so with this.
—NATHANIEL HAWTHORNE, *American Note-Books*

CASSIOPE. See under HEATH

CASTOR OIL PLANT, originally native to Africa and Asia, was cultivated in Europe untold centuries ago and then brought to America for cultivation, where it ultimately escaped hither and yon and now grows wild in our warm climates.

Kastor is the Greek word for beaver and is related to the earlier Sanskrit *kasturi*, or musk. The animal was given that name because beaver musk, or castoreum, was a valued commodity, used not only as a perfume base, but also as a cathartic in ancient medicine. Since the oil of the castor bean was similarly used as a cathartic, it was given its name from the beaver.

Nowadays, besides its continuing medical fame, castor oil is commercially produced as a lubricant for machinery, a dressing for leather, and as an ingredient in brake fluids, paints, and plastics.

As I drove out from Los Angeles into the country on a January morning with a friend . . . around us the air was musical with the sweet sound of the baa-ing of young lambs. Surely there is no prettier or kindlier sight in the world than a great flock of peaceful ewes, with their lambs, covering a plain of soft green as far as the eye can reach. All the fence corners, where there were fences, were crowded with castor-oil plant, which is here a perennial, twenty feet high—a weed whose brilliant crimson seed-pods shine like jewels in the sunlight . . . a plant, which is with us in the

East, a tender ornamental shrub.—CHARLES NORDHOFF, *California: for Health, Pleasure, and Residence,* 1872

C A T A W B A—A native American grape, pale red with a lilac bloom, a musky flavor, very juicy, very sweet, and highly aromatic.

Catawba was the name of an Indian tribe who were members of the Sioux nation and lived in the Carolinas. The word was originally *katapa* and meant "to be separate"—that is to say, the Catawba's country was separate from the other Sioux who lived largely in the west on the Great Plains. Like their western brothers, the Catawbas were famed as warriors and in the 1600's sent many large war parties against rival tribes in the Ohio valley. By the mid-1700's they had been decimated both in battle and by the white man's smallpox. Meanwhile, their name—the "separate" tribe—was given to the Catawba River on which they lived, to the catawba rhododendron, and to the catawba grape.

Among our pioneer horticulturists was Nicholas Longworth, an Ohio lawyer, who experimented with the cultivation of the catawba and with wine-making early in the 1800's and became internationally famous as the "father of American grape culture." A gift of catawba wine was sent by Mr. Longworth, from his vine-

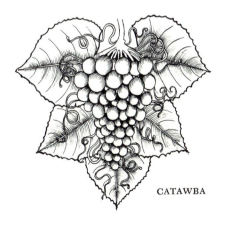

CATAWBA

yards on the Ohio River, to Henry Wadsworth Longfellow in Boston. The wine evoked a paean of delight. Here are a few of Longfellow's stanzas.

It is not a song
Of the Scuppernong,
From warm Carolinian valleys,
Nor the Isabel
And the Muscadel
That bask in our garden alleys.

Nor the red Mustang,
Whose clusters hang
O'er the waves of the Colorado,
And the fiery flood
Of whose purple blood
Has a dash of Spanish bravado.

For the richest and best
Is the wine of the West,
That grows by the beautiful river;
Whose sweet perfume
Fills all the room
With a benison on the giver.

Very good in its way
Is the Verzenay,
Or Sillery soft and creamy;
But Catawba wine
Has a taste more divine,
More dulcet, delicious, and dreamy.
—HENRY WADSWORTH LONGFELLOW, 1807–1882,
Catawba Wine

CATCHFLY. See CAMPION

CELANDINE, a butter yellow member of the butter-cup family, was given its name from the Greek word for swallow—*chelidon*. As Pliny explains this, the swallows first discovered the virtues of the plant and used the juices to cure the eye infections of their young. In fact, wrote Pliny, the power of the plant was so great that the sight of blinded swallows could be restored with a poultice of celandine. Other early writers tell us, more simply, that the celandine was so named because it blooms when the swallows arrive and fades when the swallows depart.

Nonetheless, its reputation as a restorative for fading eyesight lasted well into the 1700's, and one of its old-fashioned names was sightwort. What's more, it was also recommended for falling teeth, freckles, warts, ringworm, exema, and "the itch." Two varieties (the greater and lesser celandines) brought to the New World and planted in colonial herb gardens, ran rampant and are now among our most common American wildflowers. Most gardeners look upon the greater celandine as a pest and weed it out, but it will persist, even in the poorest soil and the darkest corners of the garden. I welcome it, in just such places. As for its persistance, I found a cluster of fresh green celandine leaves hatching under the snow and ice—yesterday, January 26.

Greater Celandine. It is one of the plants that have faithfully followed the footsteps of man, or that man has carried with him in his wanderings. We find it lurking about old farmsteads and along roads near long-settled towns rather than in more secluded localities. Any frequenter of the countryside must know the plant, especially if he has attempted to gather the cheerful blossoms and so has had his fingers badly stained with the ill-smelling yellow juice with which the stems are stored. But it is no good for cutting in any case, for leaves and flowers wilt almost immediately. It is pretty, however, and especially noticeable in early spring. —Louise Beebe Wilder, *What Happens in My Garden*, 1935

Lesser Celandine. The three lawns—they used to be lawns—have long since blossomed out into meadows filled with every sort of pretty weed. And under and among the groups of leafless oaks and beeches were blue hepaticas, white anemones, violets, and celandines in sheets. The celandines in particular delighted me with their clean, happy brightness, so beautifully trim and newly var-

nished, as though they had had painters at work on them.—Elizabeth, Countess Russell, *Elizabeth and Her German Garden*,
1898

CENTAURY. See Knapweed

CHICKWEED was given its name because birds and
chickens relish the seeds and the young foliage. And always have.
The ancient Latin name for it was *Morsus gallinae*, meaning a
morsel or a bite for hens. In German it is *Vogelkraut*, the "bird
plant"; in French *Mouron des Oiseaux*, or more simply nowadays,
Mouron—a bite, a morsel for the birds; and in England it has such
nicknames as chick wittles (that is, victuals), chicken's meat, and
cluckweed. Gerard in his *Herbal*, 1597, wrote: "Little birds in
cadges, especially Linnets, are refreshed with the lesser Chickweed when they loath their meate."

Chickweed, in its many varieties, abounds round the world in
the temperate zone—wet or dry ground, woods, fields, the cracks
in city pavements. Common chickweed and mouse-ear chickweed,
probably the most prevalent in America, are both European migrants.

On one occasion, landing on a small uninhabited island nearly
at the Antipodes, the first evidence I met with of its having been
previously visited was the English chickweed; and this I traced to
a mount that marked the grave of a British sailor, and that was
covered with the plant, doubtless the offspring of seed that had
adhered to the spade or mattock with which the grave had been
dug.—Sir Joseph Hooker, 1817–1911

Even in midwinter, if you know its haunt in some sunny nook,
you may dig away the snow, and pick its white, starry blossoms,
larger and fuller now than those of summer. I recall a beautiful
episode from one of my winter walks long ago. . . . I was skirting
the borders of a swamp where every hollow between mound and
tussock was roofed with thin, glassy ice left high and dry by the
receding of the water beneath . . . one portion of the clear crystal

40

roof disclosed a lush growth of the chickweed beneath, its starry blossoms rivalling the surrounding snow in whiteness. A mimic conservatory—no, not a mimic, rather say the *model*, the "cold-frame" which nursed its winter blossoms eons before the modern infringement of the florist was conceived of . . . —WILLIAM HAMILTON GIBSON, *Sharp Eyes*, 1892

C I N Q U E F O I L, like chickweed, is a multitudinous international family and can be found almost anywhere in the arctic and north temperate zones. The word is French, *cinque* for five and *foil* for leave—the five-leafed plant—and comes from the early Latin, *quinquefolium*, with similar old names in any number of other languages, such as *cinco en rama* in Spanish and *Fünffingerkraut* in German. Five-fingered grass was an early English nickname. In America we have a host of native cinquefoils, as well as the inevitable migrants from Europe. Some members of the family, however, such as the purple marsh cinquefoil and the bushy yellow cinquefoil, are native throughout the world—an indigenous species from California to New Jersey, from Iceland across Europe and Asia, and on to Japan. Pliny recommended

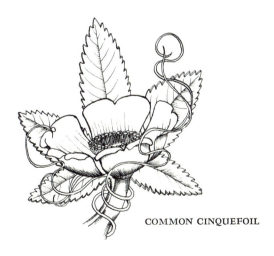

COMMON CINQUEFOIL

cinquefoil, honey, and axle-grease as an ointment for scrofula. Linnaeus gave these plants the botanic designation *Potentilla*, from the Latin *potens*, or powerful, because of their repute as powerful cure-alls.

When I was a boy I was told that certain common little yellow flowers I saw growing close to the ground in pastures and other places were "yellow strawberry blossoms" and, being more interested in baseball than botany at the time, it never occurred to me to question the matter. Furthermore, I did note a general "strawberry look" in the shape and flower, which made the misinformation easy to swallow and digest. It was years before I learned that I had been botanically bilked and the little five-petaled yellow flowers were cinquefoils, or five-fingers, of some kind, probably the Common Cinquefoil, which is the most abundant of the five or six kinds found in our region, as the Rough-fruited Cinquefoil probably is the tallest and bushiest of the group. . . . If I had known enough to look closer in my younger days, I would have noticed that the strawberry leaflets come in threes and not in the fives—or sometimes more—that mark the cinquefoil clan.
—John Kieran, *A Natural History of New York City*, 1959

C L I N T O N I A is a family name popularly used for a variety of small springtime lilies that grow in American woodlands. One of the eastern clintonias is sometimes called cornlily, because of its corn-yellow bell-like flowers that often bloom seven to a stalk. A white clintonia with an umbel of fragrant flowers, dotted in green and purple, grows in the southern Appalachians. There's a red clintonia in the redwood regions of northern California. A rare single-flowered clintonia, found at three thousand to six thousand feet in the Sierras and north in British Columbia, has two pretty nicknames—queen's cup and bride's bonnet. All of these share the nickname of beadlily, because of their deep blue seeds which look like polished lapis-lazuli.

Curiously, clintonia had no official botanic designation until early in the 1800's when it was given its name in honor of De-Witt Clinton (1796–1828), the Governor of New York. Thoreau later complained about this choice in his journal: "Clintonia borealis, amid the Solomon's-seal in Hubbard's Grove Swamp, a very neat and handsome liliaceous flower, with three large, regular, spotless green, convallaria leaves . . . four dropping, greenish-yellow, bell-shaped flowers . . . But Gray should not have named it for the Governor of New York. What is he to the lovers of flowers in Massachusetts? . . . Name your canals and railroads after Clinton, if you please, but his name is not associated with flowers."

Thoreau, however, was wrong on two counts. DeWitt Clinton, above and beyond his political career, was an ardent naturalist and published books on natural history and the natural sciences. The choice was fitting. Further, it was not Professor Asa Gray who chose the name. In his *Manual of Botany*, Gray gave the credit to Samuel Constantine Rafinesque—French-born, a naturalist, and a teacher at Transylvania University in Lexington, Kentucky. As described by those who knew him, Rafinesque was a lone, friendless, bizarre little creature, utterly absent-minded, always forgetting to eat his meals, comb his hair, or wash his face, always off in search of new species (mammals, mollusks, plants), dressed in muddy, tattered clothes. But, he never forgot to take his umbrella on a collecting expedition.

Audubon, who poked fun at Rafinesque in a memoir, *The Eccentric Naturalist*, described him as an "odd fish" who arrived on a surprise visit in "a long loose coat of yellow nankeen, much the worse for the many rubs it has got in its time and stained all over with the juice of plants. . . . His beard was as long as I have known my own to be during some of my peregrinations, and his lank black hair hung loosely over his shoulders." And in another passage, when Rafinesque came upon a new flower: "He plucked the plants one after another, danced, hugged me in my arms . . ." Audubon thought Rafinesque had gone mad and was delighted when his visitor disappeared into the western wilderness one morning before dawn, without so much as a word of farewell.

Rafinesque died in 1840, impoverished and alone in Philadelphia, amid the confusion of his precious specimens and the copies of his nine hundred and thirty books and pamphlets. These were sold for junk, and Rafinesque was buried in Potter's Field. Remember him when you find clintonia in bloom.

Red Clintonia. Its large leaves, of a rich polished green, arrange themselves symmetrically around the short stem, seeming to come from the ground—and so fine are they, that if no blossom appeared, we should feel the plant had fulfilled its mission of beauty. But in April a blossom-stalk shoots up from their midst, bearing upon its summit a cluster of deep rose-colored, nodding bells. . . . I remember a beautiful spot upon the Lagunitas Creek, where the stream, flowing over a brown, pebbly bottom, passes among the redwoods where their tall shafts make dim cathedral aisles. Here little yellow violets and the charming wood-sorrel carpet the ground, the fetid adder's-tongue spreads its mottled leaves, while groups of the lovely Clintonia put the finishing touches to an already beautiful scene.—Mary Elizabeth Parsons, *Wild Flowers of California*, 1900

C O H O S H, or Bugbane. See under Bane

C O L T S F O O T is another European emigré that's been making its way across the United States for at least two hundred years. But it was not mentioned in wildflower books until quite recently, except for Mrs. William Starr Dana, who wrote in the 1890's about her difficulties in identifying the strange plant she found growing in the Berkshires. I first became aware of coltsfoot many years ago when I found a patch of it blooming along a river in northwestern Connecticut, and the next time I saw it was high in the Alleghanies; masses of coltsfoot were blooming in the clay and gravel on the roadsides, long before the trees were even in bud.

The name coltsfoot was given in England to describe the heart-shaped leaf, and other old-time names were horse-foot, bull-foot, and foal-foot. The plant is a tried and true cough remedy of long standing. More than nineteen centuries ago, Pliny wrote: "Its root is placed on live coals of cypress wood, and the fumes of it inhaled through a funnel for chronic cough." In 1972, Adrienne Crowhurst made a comparable suggestion in *The Weed Cookbook* with a recipe for coltsfoot coughdrops. Simmer cut up rootstocks, barely covered with water, until tender. Add two cups of sugar, boil till syrupy. Put the syrup-coated bits of root to dry on wax paper and let harden.

There is coltsfoot to consider, a plant used for centuries as a homespun remedy for colds. Indeed, the generic name Tussilago is derived from the Latin word for cough, *tussis* . . . The belief in its medical benefits came with it from overseas and I remember cough drops and candy canes flavored with Coltsfoot that were sold in country stores. With a sugar coating, this was a medicine that went down easily with children . . . The plant itself is much misunderstood. There is no doubt that many persons who see great patches of the low-growing yellow flower heads in early spring mistake them for dandelions of some kind. Of course, a close look at the smaller heads on woolly stems made up of overlapping segments would dispel the idea that they were dandelions, but most persons give only a casual glance at such flowers. The plant thrives on moist banks in sun or shade and blooms in profusion on the sloping sides of vacant lots in outlying sections of the city.—JOHN KIERAN, *A Natural History of New York City*, 1959

C O L U M B I N E, from the Latin *columba* or dove, means dove-like, and the name was given because the flowers resemble a circle of doves; the long nectaries are the heads and shoulders of the birds and the flaring petals the birds' wings. Columbina, or "little dove," was a pet name in Italian once upon a time for one's lady love. Thus, in the Commedia dell'Arte, Harlequin's beloved was Columbine.

In religious art, the columbine was likened to a white dove and symbolized the Holy Ghost. A stalk of columbine with seven blooms was symbolic of the seven gifts of the Holy Ghost, according to Isaiah 11:2—the spirit of the Lord, the spirits of wisdom,

understanding, counsel, might, knowledge, and the fear of the Lord.

The American Indians made infusions of columbine seeds for headaches and fevers. In Colorado, where the wide mountain meadows of the Rockies explode with blue and white columbine in early summer, it is protected as the state flower. Our other native species are scarlet and yellow, yellow, and lavender and yellow. But whether wild or nursery-bred, European or American, columbine—like the daisy and the rose—is one of the most beloved of flowers and has evoked miles of poetry and prose. As John Parkinson put it, over three hundred years ago, "Columbines are flowers of that respect as that no Garden would willingly be without them."

Although under cultivation the columbine nearly doubles its size, it never has the elfin charm in a conventional garden that it possesses wild in Nature's. Dancing in red and yellow petticoats, to the rhythm of the breeze, along the ledge of overhanging rocks, it coquettes with some Punchinello as if daring him to reach her at his peril.—NELTJE BLANCHAN, *Nature's Garden*, 1901

"Is it not afraid?" asked a little child who saw the columbine as it was bent and swayed by the wind over a rocky cliff, and appeared to cling so lightly to the crumbled soil. "No," was the answer, "the columbine has a fearless heart and a spirited courage: it is never afraid."—ALICE LOUNSBERRY, *A Guide to the Wild Flowers*, 1899

. . . those particular combinations of tints that are supplied to a May garden by its columbines—maroon and saffron, lemon and rusty pink, sapphire blue and water white, colors gay yet drowned by time passing and gradually immersing them.—SIR OSBERT SITWELL, *Right Hand, Left Hand*, 1946

Be very shy of double flowers; choose the old Columbine where the clustering doves are unmistakable and distinct, not the double one, where they run into mere tatters.—WILLIAM MORRIS, 1834–1896

COMPASS-PLANT grows in our central and southern states. The name refers to the north–south direction in which the young leaves tend to align. Hence, the flower's other common nickname of polar plant. In 1777, William Bartram, then traveling through Cherokee country along the Mobile River, described a variety of compass plant as "the most conspicuous, both for

COMPASS PLANT

beauty and novelty. . . . The flower stem, which is eight or ten feet in length, terminates upwards with a long heavy spike of large golden yellow flowers." The stems, when split "exude a resinous substance, which the sun and air harden in semi-pellucid drops or tears of a pale amber colour. This resin possesses a very agreeable fragrance and bitterish taste, somewhat like frankincense or turpentine; it is chewed by the Indians and traders, to cleanse their teeth and mouth, and sweeten their breath."

In 1866, a report from Nebraska filed with the Department of Agriculture in Washington, noted: "Horses fed up on hay, with polar plant intermixed, are never known to have the heaves. Cattle, sheep, mules and horses, are extremely fond of the heads of the plant while green, as well as when mixed with hay. The pure white resinous gum which they contain performs radical cures in all bronchial cases."

"Patience!" the priest would say: "Have faith, and thy prayers will
    be answered.
Look at this delicate plant that lifts its head from the meadow;
See how its leaves are turned to the north, as true as the magnet—
This is the compass-flower, that the finger of God has planted
Here in the houseless wild, to direct the traveller's journey.
                              —HENRY WADSWORTH LONGFELLOW,
                                  Evangeline, 1847

Every July I watch eagerly a certain country graveyard that I pass in driving to and from my farm. . . . It is an ordinary graveyard, bordered by the usual spruces and studded with the usual pink granite or white marble headstones, each with the usual Sunday bouquet or red of pink geraniums. It is extraordinary only in being triangular instead of square, and in harboring, within the sharp angle of its fence, a pin-point remnant of the native prairie on which the graveyard was established in the 1840's. Heretofore unreachable by scythe or mower, this yard-square relic of original Wisconsin gives birth, each July, to a man-high stalk of compass plant . . . spangled with saucer-sized yellow blooms resembling sunflowers. It is the sole remnant of this plant along this highway, and perhaps the sole remnant in the western half of our county.

48

What a thousand acres of compass plant looked like when they tickled the bellies of the buffalo is a question never again to be answered, and perhaps not even asked.—ALDO LEOPOLD, *A Sand County Almanac*, 1949

C O R E O P S I S—We tend to think of the coreopsis as an old-fashioned garden flower. Rarely as a wildflower. But the coreopsis is a native of North and South America that's been cultivated since its discovery, cross-bred, coaxed and admired, and was returned to us from European horticulturists in new and surprising variations.

The name is Greek, given by Linnaeus, and means "resembling a bedbug"—*from koris*, bedbug, and *opsis* sight or appearance. And where, you may well ask, did Linnaeus see bedbugs in these American wildflowers? In the dark seeds which have two small feeler-like horns. But not only is the seed a good imitation of the bedbug, it also looks like a tick—depending, of course, on your frame of reference—and tickseed is a common nickname.

In garden catalogues, the cultivated varieties of coreopsis are usually listed by the more becoming name of calliopsis, which roughly translates into "it has a beautiful appearance." Again, the root words are Greek; *kallos*, beauty, and *opsis*, sight or appearance.

Anyone seeking a clear-cut path through the jungle of Coreopsis history could be pardoned for giving up the task, since this self-reliant group is scattered over both hemispheres and has wandered hither and thither interminably. Wild species have been cultivated and cultivated ones have taken off into the wild for many ages.

A typical coreopsis is quite indifferent about where it grows. Railroad embankments, gravel pits, and all kinds of areas where the ground has been disturbed by grading operations suit it admirably. Country roadsides are specially favored spots. In fact, there is evidence that many of the plants have made their way inland from the coast by simply following recently built high-

49

ways whose shoulders have been graded and left in a more or less raw state. . . . They have a happy faculty of lasting unusually long when cut and placed in water.—ROBERT S. LEMMON, *Wildflowers of North America*, 1961

One could go about gathering an enormous yellow bouquet out of the heart of July. Fill the arms with orange lilies, the ubiquitous gold; sweep up the sunflowers, the gold honeysuckle, the great stalky suns of compass plants and prairie dock; find clumps of black-eyed Susans rimmed with gold, and wild coreopsis . . . —JOSEPHINE W. JOHNSON, *The Inland Island*, 1969

CORNFLOWER. See KNAPWEED

CORYDALIS—The only nickname I know for these delicate spring flowers is fume-root, given because of the curious nitrous odor of the roots. Otherwise, in most wildflower books, it is listed only under its scientific name, corydalis. This name was given to the purple and the yellow European varieties by Johann Jakob Dillenius (1687–1747), the first professor of botany at Oxford.

When Linnaeus visited England, he went to the university to present his new system of plant classification to the aged and venerable professor. Dillenius' initial reaction was one of shock. He is said to have stalked angrily into the library, and pointing back to Linnaeus whom he had left in the garden, Dillenius exclaimed, "There goes the man who is bringing all botany into confusion." Linnaeus, however, won the professor over and by the end of his visit, Dillenius begged the young Swedish botanist to stay at Oxford and share his salary. But Linnaeus had other plans for his life and returned to Europe to publish *Genera Plantarum*, and, in classifying corydalis, he used the name Dillenius had chosen earlier.

Corydalis (the accent is on the second syllable) is a Greek word meaning crested lark, *korydallis*, from *korys*, or helmet—given in reference to the nectary, which is spurred like the claw of the lark. (See LARKSPUR.) The Sino-Himalayas are said to be the place where the most extravagant varieties of corydalis can be found. In America we have several kinds growing on the eastern seaboard from Canada to Georgia. In Indian medicine, the roots of golden corydalis were steamed on hot coals and the smoke inhaled to clear the head of a cold or congestion.

June 6, 1853. Corydalis glauca, a delicate glaucous plant rarely met with, with delicate flesh-colored and yellow flowers, covered with a glaucous bloom, on dry rocky hills. Perhaps it suggests gentility. Set it down as early as middle of May or earlier.—HENRY DAVID THOREAU, 1817–1862, *Journals*

It is the destiny of certain plants to make the world in which they live a pleasanter and more gracious place. Indeed it is such as these that often endow a garden with peculiar charm. Like mist in the distance they soften and enhance the landscape, bestow grace and a little sense of mystery. . . . As I consider this type of plant there comes to mind certain Corydalis, lovely in shadowed walls . . . —LOUISE BEEBE WILDER, *What Happens in My Garden*, 1935

C O W B A N E, or Water Hemlock. See under BANE

C O W S L I P—Such a pretty pastoral name for a flower, but if you take a second look, it's nothing more than a barnyard name. In Anglo-Saxon the word was *cuslyppe, cu* for cow, and *slyppe* for slop. So cowslip, with no fol-de-rol whatsoever, means cow-slop or cow-dung. There are comparable words, for example, in Old Danish and Icelandic with similar meanings. Presumably these names were given because cowslips flourish in cow pastures.

In England the cowslip is the common primrose, with soft yellow flowers and crinkled leaves in a rosette, that grows wild not only in English meadows but throughout northern Europe and across the meadowlands of Russia.

In America the name was passed on to the Virginia bluebell, which is often called the Virginia cowslip. Shooting stars, the

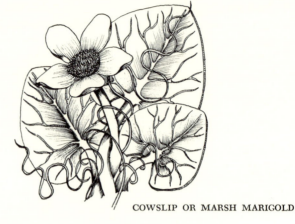

COWSLIP OR MARSH MARIGOLD

little wild plant that looks so much like cyclamen, is known as the American cowslip. But we hear cowslip most frequently as a name for our marsh marigolds, which bloom early in the spring, one of our first flowers after the ice has broken. Among certain of the northeastern Indians, the marsh marigold was known as the flower that "opens the swamps."

The leaves have always been known as good eating—gathered in May before they tend to get bitter. But a word of warning: They should always be cooked, because even the young leaves are acrid in their raw state. The buds can be pickled to use as capers, and a fine wine can be made from the glossy yellow blossoms.

> *Brook Farm. May 4, 1841.* . . . I look beneath the stone-walls, where the verdure is richest, in hopes that a little company of violets, or some solitary bud, prophetic of the summer, may be there. . . . But not a wild-flower have I yet found. One of the boys gathered some yellow cowslips last Sunday; but I am well content not to have found them for they are not precisely what I should like to send you, though they deserve honor and praise, because they come to us when no others will.—NATHANIEL HAWTHORNE, to his fiancée, Miss Sophia Peabody

Down in the moist green swamp lot the yellow cowslips bloom

along the shallow ditch, and the eager farmer's wife fills her basket with the succulent leaves she has been watching for so long; for they'll tell you in New England that "they ain't noth'n' like caowslips for a mess o' greens."—W. HAMILTON GIBSON, *Pastoral Days*, 1880

These flowers are peddled about our streets every spring under the name of cowslips—a title to which they have no claim . . . the result of that reckless fashion of christening unrecognized flowers, which is responsible for so much confusion about their English names.—MRS. WILLIAM STARR DANA, *How to Know the Wild-Flowers*, 1893

C R A N B E R R Y—The name for these low, creeping, bog plants comes from the Old German *Kranbere*, or crane-berry, and was given because the long stamens of the flowers resemble the beak of a crane. They are members of the HEATH family and indigenous both to northern Europe and North America. The American high-bush cranberry, by the way, is not related; it belongs to the honeysuckle family.

Even before American planters began to cultivate the cranberry commercially, early in the 1800's, the wild berries were gathered and sold as a market crop, and quantities of cranberry preserves were shipped to Europe and the West Indies. American cranberry vines were then introduced to England as "a plant of easy culture, and with but little expense, meadows which are now barren wastes might be converted into profitable cranberry fields. Any meadow will answer."

A tea of cranberry leaves was popular with the Ojibways as a cure for nausea.

Cranberry, or bearberry (because bears use much to feed upon them), is a small, trayling plant, that grows in salt marshes that are overgrown with moss. The tender branches, which are reddish, run out in great length, lying flat on the ground. . . . The leaves are like box, but greener—thick and glistering. The blossoms are very like the flowers of our English night-shade; after which

53

succeed the berries, hanging by long, small foot-stalks, no bigger than a hair. At first, they are of a pale-yellow colour; afterwards red, and as big as a cherry . . . of a sower, astringent taste. They are excellent against the scurvy. They are also good to allay the fervour of hot diseases. The Indians and English use them much, boyling them with sugar for sauce to eat with their meat; and it is a delicate sauce, especially for roasted mutton.—JOHN JOSSE-LYN, *New England's Rarities Discovered*, 1672

And in peaty soil on headlands above the bay when the air is crisp with a foretaste of fall, one finds the slow-ripening highland cranberries that can be cooked into a more tangy, tart, delicious sauce than the Cape Cod cranberry has ever made. Intermingling with the heathery crowberry, the cranberry bushes form a closely woven, springy mat, which smooths over all the lesser irregularities of the rough ground. Upon arriving at such a place, the picker is tempted to forget the berries, to stretch out in the heathy, sour fragrance and the relaxing warmth of the sun, and give up all purposes, surrendering to the indulgence of his senses. Who says that to dream away an afternoon with a foam-streaked bay spread out before your half-shut eyes and a wind stroking your face is not as purifying as gathering a small basket of bullet-hard berries for cranberry jelly?—ELIOT PORTER, *Summer Island*, 1966

CRANESBILL. See GERANIUM

CREEPING CHARLIE, or CREEPING LOOSESTRIFE. See MONEYWORT

DAISY is the "day's eye" and was named by the Anglo-Saxons—*daeges eye*. But the name was not given because of the white rays and yellow heart of the flower, like an image of the sun. It was given because the little pink and white English daisy

OX-EYE DAISY

closes at nightfall and opens again at sunrise. Thus, it is the eye of the day. The ox-eye daisy, the most common variety in American fields, came to us from England, where there is an old saying that spring has not arrived till you can set your foot on twelve daisies. White weed and May weed are two of its early nicknames, and as a "weed," daisies are not loved by everyone. The Farmer's Encyclopedia, in 1851, sourly described them as "gawky-looking flowers, and notwithstanding their celebration by poets, daisies are a blemish in a neat grassplot."

Daisies belong to the composite family (*Compositae*) along with dandelions, sunflowers, thistles, asters, marigolds, goldenrod, hawkweed, and the like. I was amazed when I first learned about composites. Consider the daisy, for example. What appears to be *one* flower is actually many, many flowers. Each white "petal" is an individual flower, and the yellow center is made up of innumerable tiny tubular florets. The white rays are adapted to attract pollinating insects and to give them a landing platform, while the yellow florets contain both the stamens and the pistils. When you pick a daisy, you are, in truth, picking a cluster of flowers—a veritable bouquet.

If you dream of daisies in spring or summer, it's a sign of good luck. But to dream of them in fall or winter is a sign of bad luck. What's more, if you eat the roots of daisies, they will stunt your growth, but if you eat three heads of daisies after having a tooth pulled, you will never have a toothache again.

The pastoral writers of other countries appear as if they had paid nature an occasional visit . . . but the British poets have lived and revelled with her—they have wooed her in her most secret haunts— they have watched her minutest caprices. A spray could not tremble in the breeze—a leaf could not rustle to the ground—a diamond drop could not patter in the stream—nor a daisy unfold its crimson tints to the morning, but it has been noticed by these impassioned and delicate observers, and wrought up into some beautiful morality.—WASHINGTON IRVING, *The Sketch Book*, 1820

June 18, 1835. A walk in North Salem in the decline of yesterday afternoon. . . . The verdure, both of trees and grass, is now in its prime, the leaves elastic, all life. The grass-fields are plentously bestrewn with white-weed, large spaces looking as white as a sheet of snow, at a distance, yet with an indescribably warmer tinge than snow,—living white, intermixed with living green. —NATHANIEL HAWTHORNE, *American Note-Books*

Myriads and myriads of daisies, whitening our fields as if a belated blizzard had covered them with a snowy mantle in June, fill the farmer with dismay, the flower-lover with rapture. . . . Now, what is the secret of the large, white daisy's triumphal conquest? A naturalized immigrant from Europe and Asia, how could it so quickly take possession? In the over-cultivated Old World no weed can have half the chance for unrestricted colonizing that is has in our vast unoccupied area. Once released . . . they find life here easy, pleasant; as if to make up for lost time, they increase a thousandfold. . . . Small wonder that our fields are white with daisies. A long and merry life to them!—NELTJE BLANCHAN, *Nature's Garden*, 1901

DAME'S ROCKET, which is native to Europe and Asia, is yet another foreign flower that has naturalized itself on the far side of the garden wall and is now listed in American wildflower guides. At the turn of the century, Alice Morse Earle wrote of seeing it occasionally in secluded spots along New England roadsides. Nowadays, you can find dame's rocket in profusion, blooming inland as far as Iowa. In fact, you are more apt to find it growing wild these days. It seems to be one of those old-fashioned garden flowers that have gone out of style, except for the double hybrid varieties.

Dame's rocket blooms early in the summer, tall and fragrant, in pink and white. To the hasty eye, it appears to be phlox. But look again. The phlox have five petals. Dame's rocket, which belongs to the MUSTARD family, has four. The name is an approximate translation of its Latin name, *Hesperis matronalis*, which had been in use since the middle ages and was officially chosen as the plant's designation in the 1600's by Joseph Pitton de Tournefort, the French botanist. The word *hesperis* means "pertaining to the evening," because the flowers are at their sweetest during the evening hours, and *matronalis* comes from *matrona*, meaning a lady, a wife, a matron. All of which is a clumsy way of saying that the blooms, known for their evening fragrance, were particularly associated with a woman's flower garden, as opposed to an herb garden or a vegetable garden. It has been said, for example, that dame's rocket was Marie Antoinette's favorite flower.

Other English names for *Hesperis matronalis* are damewort, dame's violet, and sweet rocket. Rocket, by the by, has no special interpretation as a flower name. It's the English version of *eruca,* a Latin word of no known meaning that was originally used for this plant in ancient times.

June 3. The rockets are all out. The gardener, in a fit of inspiration, put them right along the very front of two borders, and I don't know what his feelings can be now that they are all flowering and the plants behind are completely hidden. . . . They are charming things, as delicate in colour as in scent, and a bowl of them on my writing-table fills the room with fragrance. Single rows, however, are a mistake; I had masses of them planted in the

57

grass, and these show how lovely they can be.—ELIZABETH, COUNTESS RUSSELL, *Elizabeth and Her German Garden,* 1898

And what of the night-scented flowers? To many of us there is no time when the scents in the garden are more exquisite than at twilight. The scents of the roses and the lilies then seem sweeter than at any other hour. The scent of honeysuckle is richer, and lured by it the hawk-moths fly to extract the honey which lies too deep for the bees or wasps to reach. Nor do the jasmines exhale their richest perfumes until darkness falls, and the double white Rocket has rejoiced generations of scent-lovers with the sweetness of its perfume in the evening.—ELEANOUR SINCLAIR RHODE, *The Scented Garden,* 1931

D A N D E L I O N—"Dear common flower that grow'st beside the way, fringing the dusty road with harmless gold, first pledge of blithesome May . . ." That was James Russell Lowell speaking, though you may not share his poetic sentiments toward the dandelion. But many people do. Spring would not be spring without them. "Their lovely constellations make a little heaven on earth of the grassy places that have been brown and bare for months. They touch the heartstrings in much the same way as the early notes of the robin." Those lines come from a wildflower book written in 1902 by Frances Theodora Parsons.

The word dandelion is an anglicization of the original French name *dent de lion,* the tooth of the lion, and the name was given because of the jagged, toothlike edges of the leaves. It was also given the surprising name of *pissenlit* in French, which was carried into English as pissabed—these being a commentary on the dandelion's efficacy as a diuretic.

The common dandelion came to America from Europe and has a highly uncommon way of insuring its survival. The yellow blooms are fairly low in the grass, but as the flower head goes to seed, the dandelion puts on one last spurt of growth and lengthens the height of its stalk so that the ripened seeds will be above the grass line, up where the wind can catch them and carry them to their next breeding ground. And as all children know, dandelion clocks will tell you the time. Blow on the seed head twice and however many seeds remain give you the hour of the day. But to dream about dandelions is bad luck.

The young leaves are delicious in salads or boiled and served like spinach. The young roots, too, can be peeled and boiled as a vegetable.

Upon a showery night and still,
   Without a sound of warning,
A trooper band surprised the hill,
   And held it in the morning.

We were not waked by bugle-notes,
   No cheer our dreams invaded,
And yet, at dawn, their yellow coats
   On the green slopes paraded.

We careless folk the deed forgot;
   Till one day, idly walking,
We marked upon the self-same spot
   A crowd of veterans talking.

They shook their trembling heads and gray
   With pride and noiseless laughter;
When, well-a-day! they blew away,
   And ne'er were heard of after!
                    —HELEN GRAY CONE, 1859–1934,
                                    Dandelions

I used to think that this wine was just another of the clever concoctions invented by Americans in the twenties to evade prohibition, but now I find that Dandelion Wine has been made and appreciated in England for many generations. . . . My "drinking uncle" says that, even during the worst blizzard in January, a glass of Dandelion Wine will bring summer right into the house.
—EUELL GIBBONS, *Stalking the Wild Asparagus*, 1962

DAYFLOWER and DAY LILY—These names mean that the flowers last for only one day, an explanation that seems almost simple-minded if you know about dayflowers and

DAY LILY

day lilies. But if you don't, you could be in for a surprise, as I was once many years ago when I arranged a spectacular bouquet of orange day lilies in a pewter bowl, and at sundown found I had a bedraggled bouquet of limp and dying flowers.

The tawny orange variety are scentless, the yellow ones—also called lemon lilies or custard lilies—are sweet. Both originated in East Asia and came to America by way of European gardens. Here they have run wild. Sun, shade, sand, woodland soil, tarmac—they will grow almost anywhere, and do, a beautiful, bright addition to our landscape, though they will take over the garden given half a chance. They like our climate, our long hot summers. But in a misty climate they must be carefully fostered. I was invited once upon a time into an Irish garden to see the lilies in bloom. They turned out to be our wild day lilies, the self-same breed that so many American gardeners treat as a pest and weed out by the bushelbasket full. The score was balanced, however. Irish pastures were purple with foxglove.

The word lily, by the way, has no known translation. It was *lilium* in Latin, *leirion* in Greek, and there the line stops.

Of the several kinds of day-lilies seen in gardens, none equals the old-fashioned and always beautiful "yellow lily." My garden was already generously stocked with this favorite plant, when, driving in the country, I saw two such uncommonly fine clumps growing in the unmown grass of a farm-yard, that the remembrance of them haunted me for days. I had not peace of mind until I should secure them. How they would light the front border! An exchange for a dozen rose-bushes was the inducement I held out to the old lady who owned the coveted plants—and the huge clumps, which one man could scarcely lift, were duly transferred to a post of honor. They threw up three spikes of bloom the following season! Perhaps they missed the chanticleer of the farm-yard to waken them into bloom; perhaps they mourned the old lady's absence who had planted them and watched them and smelled them and complimented them. . . . Who knows? (I may add that the plants have become re-established, and now flower with their former luxuriance.)—George H. Ellwanger, *The Garden's Story*, 1889

The dayflower, which many gardeners also look upon as a pest, has a pretty three-petaled face. In American species, all the petals are blue. In the Asiatic variety, now wild in this country, the two top petals are blue and the bottom one white. Their scientific name is *Commelina*, and they were named by Linnaeus after a family of early Dutch botanists, the Commelin brothers. As the story goes, the choice was Linnaeus' private joke. The two blue petals at the top represented the two Commelin brothers who were dedicated scientists and ornaments to their profession. The small white petal at the base of the flower memorialized the third brother who never amounted to much. Happily, the worthless brother had died before Linnaeus published this botanical dig in his *Species Plantarum*, and never knew that he was thus immortalized.

In the morning we find the day-flower open and alert-looking, owing to the sharp, erect bracts that give it support; after noon, or as soon as it has been fertilized by the female bees that are its chief benefactors, while collecting its abundant pollen, the lovely petals roll up, never to open again, and quickly wilt into a wet, shapeless mass, which, if we touch it, leaves a sticky blue fluid on our fingertips.—Neltje Blanchan, *Nature's Garden*, 1901

DELPHINIUM. See LARKSPUR

DEVIL'S-BIT, DEVIL'S-PAINTBRUSH.
See HAWKWEED

DEVIL'S-TRUMPET. See JIMSONWEED

DITTANY, one of the many mints, was named by the
Greeks—*diktamnon*; that is to say, a plant abundant on Mt. Dicto
in Crete. According to ancient legend, wild goats living on the
island of Crete would seek out and eat dittany if they had been
wounded with javelins, and the arrowheads would fall immediately from their flesh. In the Aeneid, Virgil wrote that Venus used
this herb to cure Aeneas' battle wounds.

> A branch of healing dittany she brought,
> Which in the Cretan fields with care she sought . . .
> Well known to wounded goats; a sure relief
> To draw the pointed steel, and ease the grief.

By the year 1597, when John Gerard wrote his *Herbal,* the
power ascribed to dittany was even greater than in Virgil's day. "It
prevaileth much against all wounds, and especially those made
with invenomed weapons, arrowes shot out of guns, or such like,
and is very profitable for Chirurgians [surgeons] that follow the
sea and land wars, to carry with them and have in readiness: it
draweth forth also splinters of wood, bones, or such like."

The wild dittany found in American woodlands—with its small
clusters of purple flowers typical of the mint family—is native
born.

The Horse Flies are not only a great Grievance to Horses, but
likewise to those that ride them. These little Vixons confine themselves chiefly to the Woods, and are most in moist Places. Tho'
this Insect be no bigger than an ordinary Fly, it bites very smartly,
darting its little Proboxcis into the Skin the instant it lights upon
it . . . But Dittany, which is to be had in the Woods all the

while those Insects remain in Vigor, is a sure defense against them. For this purpose, if you stick a bunch of it on the Head-Stall of your Bridle, they will be sure to keep a respectful Distance. —WILLIAM BYRD, *Histories of the Dividing Line betwixt Virginia and North Carolina*, 1728

D O D D E R means to tremble or quiver, the name given to the leafless, entwining, parasitic plants with little waxy flowers because the threadlike stalks quiver in the wind. The root word is an Old English verb, *dadiren*, to tremble, and our present-day version of the verb, to dodder, has the same connotation—to tremble, to totter, to be unsteady on one's feet.

There are several native dodders in America, as well as a few European varieties introduced over the centuries and doing very nicely in the New World. In England, where dodder was an ever-present pest in flax fields, this lethal parasite was also known as devil's gut and hellweed. Meanwhile, it was recommended in medieval medicine as cure for epilepsy, the madness caused by melancholy, the French disease (syphilis), and leprosy.

The plants emerge from the ground, each like a fine yellow

DODDER

hair, till they are an inch and a half or two inches long; they reach with might and main toward the nearest legitimate-growing plant, and when they touch it, cling like a limpet; then they draw their other end up out of the ground and set up housekeeping for the rest of their lives. They adhere to the unhappy individual upon which they have fixed themselves with a grip that grows more and more horrible; they suck all its juices, drink all its health and strength and beauty, and fling out trailers to the next, and the next, and the next, till the whole garden is a mass of ruin and despair.—CELIA THAXTER, *Among the Isles of Shoals*, 1873

We have the common Dodder, known by the people of the Southern States as "Love-Vine." It is difficult to imagine why a plant which winds itself around another, sucking the life from that which it clings to, should be suggestive of love, unless it be of that species which was in the mind of Byron when he thus apostrophized:

> "Oh, love! What is it in this world of ours
> That makes it so fatal to be loved?"
>> —THOMAS MEEHAN,
>> *The Native Flowers and Ferns of the*
>> *United States*, 1880

D O G B A N E. See under BANE

D O G - T O O T H   V I O L E T. See TROUT LILY

F A I R Y - S L I P P E R. See CALYPSO

F A W N   L I L Y. See TROUT LILY

F E R N. Here's a lovely word, adapted from the Anglo-

64

Saxon *fearn* and the German *farn* with a lineage that goes back to the Sanskrit *parna*, which originally meant a wing or feather. From this source, it became the descriptive name for the ferns, because of their feathery or plume-like leaves.

Softly they cover moist ground; unobtrusively they seek a foothold in rock crevices, mellowing the contours of cliffs and walls even as they delight the eye with their intricate patterns. . . . During the Carboniferous Period, 250 million years ago, ferns and their relatives—the giant club mosses and horsetails—were the dominant plants on earth and formed majestic forests that have not been surpassed in grandeur since then. . . . Among the 8000 species of ferns that exist today, only the tree ferns of tropical forests give an idea of what their giant ancestors were like. They tower sometimes to eighty feet . . .

From these mammoth forms members of the fern family range on down to veritable miniatures; in substance they go from the tough bracken fern to the delicate maidenhair. The leaves of most are feathery and multiple-divided, but some are merely forked like a bird's foot or are quite plain and spatula-shaped. A few are shaped like hearts or four-leaf clovers, and their leaves are held on long slender "stems." Some others are long graceful ribbons. Wherever they grow they give a dreamy quality to the scene. . . . Nature was surely in a gentle mood when she created the ferns.
—HENRY and REBECCA NORTHEN, *Ingenious Kingdom*, 1970

Going along the old Carlisle road, I perceive the grateful scent of the Dicksonia fern now partly decayed. It reminds me of all up-country with its springy mountain sides and unexhausted vigor. . . . When I wade through my narrow cow-paths it is as if I had strayed into an ancient and decayed herb garden. Nature perfumes her garments with this essence now especially. The very scent of it, if you have a decayed frond in your chamber, will take you far up-country in a twinkling. You would think you had gone after the cows there or were lost in the mountains.—HENRY DAVID THOREAU, *Journals*

The fern conceals its grace, delicacy, and beauty in the shadowed glens of the forest. Because the charm of this plant is seen only by the honest searcher, the fern symbolizes solitary humility, frankness, and sincerity.—GEORGE FERGUSON, *Signs and Symbols in Christian Art*, 1954

FIREWEED grows throughout the world in northerly climates, and in America from the sub-arctic to the mountains of Georgia. The name was not given because of its hot pink color or tall flame-like spires, but because it flourishes in ground that has been burned over. After flowering, the pods are beautiful too —bursting with silken down that flies away in the wind. If you can recognize the young shoots when they first come out of the ground, pick them, cook them, and serve like asparagus.

I overtook the Indian at the edge of some burnt land, which extended three or four miles at least . . . an exceedingly wild and desolate region. Judging by the weeds and sprouts, it appeared to have been burnt about two years before. It was covered with charred trunks, either prostrate or standing, which crocked our clothes and hands . . . and there were great fields of fireweed on all sides, the most extensive I ever saw, which presented great masses of pink.—HENRY DAVID THOREAU, *The Allegash and East Branch*, 1857

London, July 25, 1944. London, paradoxically, is the gayest

FIREWEED

where she has been most blitzed. The wounds made this summer by flying bombs are, of course, still raw and bare, but cellars and courts shattered into rubble by the German raids of 1940–41 have been taken over by an army of weeds which have turned them into wild gardens.

There is the brilliant rose-purple plant that Londoners call rose-bay willow herb. Americans call it fireweed because it blazes wherever a forest fire has raged. It will not grow in the shade, but there is little shade as yet in the London ruins. It likes potash, and the ruins are full of wood ash. It sweeps across this pock-marked city and turns what might have been scars into flaming beauty. You see it everywhere—great meadows of it in Lambeth, where solid tracts were blitzed; waves of it about St. Paul's. Behind Westminster Abbey bits of it are high up where second-story fireplaces still cling to the hanging walls.—Lewis Gannett, *New York Herald Tribune*

F L A G. See Iris

F L E A B A N E. See under Bane

F O R G E T - M E - N O T—The name is the same in French, *ne-m'oubliez-pas*, and in German, *Vergissmeinnicht*. Mouse ear is an old nickname you still hear from time to time, because of the mouse-eared leaves, and scorpion grass is another, because the raceme of pink-to-blue blossoms curls up and over in the same manner as a scorpion's tail when it strikes. In fact, there is an official scientific word for this sort of botanical curve or curl—"scorpioid." One of the most enchanting flowers in the world (and there are varieties growing worldwide), a fragrant northwestern species is the state flower of Alaska.

While wandering about the banks of these gold-besprinkled streams, I was so fortunate as to meet an interesting French Canadian, an old *coureur de bois*, who after a few minutes conversation invited me to accompany him to his gold mine on the head of Defot Creek. . . . we arrived at the cabin about the middle of the afternoon. Before entering it he threw down his burden and made haste to show me his favorite flower, a blue forget-me-not, a specimen of which he found within a few rods of the cabin, and proudly handed it to me with the finest respect, and telling its many charms and lifelong associations, showed in every endearing look and touch and gesture that the tender little plant of the mountain wildnerness was truly his best-loved darling.—JOHN MUIR, *Travels in Alaska*, 1915

As for forget-me-not legends, there are dozens of them. In ancient Egypt if you anointed your eyes with forget-me-nots during the month of Thoth, the ibis-headed god, you would see visions. In another old story, the name was said to have been given because the taste of the leaves was so sickening, you would never forget it.

According to a tale in Christian mythology, God named all the plants during the days of Creation, but there was one small blue flower that never could remember what it was called. The Lord forgave the flower's absentmindedness and whispered, "Forget-me-not. That shall be thy name."

As the story is told in an old German folk-tale, a young man finds a little blue flower in the mountains, and the flower leads him to a cave full of gold. As he stuffs his pockets with treasure, a beautiful lady appears. "Forget not the best," she warns. But the young man pays her no heed and takes only the gold, leaving the blue flower behind him—the precious forget-me-not. With that, the rocks of the mountain fall in and close the mouth of the golden cave forever.

Of all the forget-me-not legends, however, here is the one told most often in one version or another.

A fair lady and her lover, who walked by the River Danube, espied a bunch of sweet blue flowers in a steep and dangerous place. The lady asked for them, and her lover essayed to pluck a bouquet for her; but he lost his footing and fell into a deep pool. As he sank from her sight forever, he threw the beauty-wreathed flowers onto the bank and called out with his dying breath, "Forget me not . . . forget me not."—Mrs. M. L. Rayne, *Favourite Flowers*, 1882

F O X G L O V E is one of those names etymologists cannot seem to let alone. They have been trying for years to find an obscure meaning where no such obscurity exists. Rev. Walter Skeat tried to scotch this sort of thing in the 1880's in his *Etymological Dictionary of the English Language*: "A modern error, invented in 1851 by Fox Talbot, is to derive *fox-glove* from *folks'-gloves*, with the silly interpretation of *folks* as being "the good folks," or the fairies, in face of the evidence that the AS name was *foxes-glofa*=the glove of a fox." He further cited the Norwegian *revhandske*, from *rev*, a fox, and *handske*, a glove, and *revbjölla*, or foxbell.

But Rev. Skeats's efforts were in vain. One still runs across the "gloves for fairy-folk" translation. Another that pops up occasionally is "fox-music," with glove supposedly derived from *gleow*, the Anglo-Saxon word for music, since the blossoms are strung on their stalks like a string of bells; fanciful, but unfounded.

Foxglove blossoms have evoked many nicknames down through the years, such as bloody fingers, deadman's bells, ladies'-thimbles, and dog's fingers. The French choices were *gants de notre dame*, Our Lady's gloves, and *doigts de la Vierge*, the Virgin's fingers. In German the name is *Fingerhut*, finger-hat or thimble, which

FOXGLOVE

suggested to botanist Leonhard Fuchs the specific Latin designation of *digitalis*, "pertaining to the finger," when he classified this genus in the 1500's. Digitalis, of course, is familiar to all of us as a vital medicine for heart disease. Strangely enough, the foxglove's medical worth was not known to ancient or medieval physicians, although the digitalis family—some twenty-five varieties—are native to Europe and Central Asia. Foxglove surfaced as a folk medicine in the 1700's, when a Dr. William Withering of Shropshire took notice of its use in the miraculous cures wrought by an aged herb woman. The American Indians, however, had always used our native yellow "false foxglove" as a cardiac stimulant.

Among the true foxgloves, the common red-purple variety has escaped our gardens and naturalized itself in scattered areas across North America.

June, 1918. Always, when I see foxgloves, I think of the L.'s. Again I pass in front of their cottage and in the window, between the daffodil curtains with the green spots—there are the great sumptuous blooms.

"And how beautiful they are against the white-wash!" cry the L.'s. As is their custom, when they love anything, they make a sort of Festa. With foxgloves everywhere. And then they sit in the middle of them, like blissful prisoners, dining in an encampment of Indian Braves.—KATHERINE MANSFIELD, *Journal*

When we dropped from the high Cascades into the valley of the Columbia River just above Bonneville Dam, we saw growing beside the road clumps of magenta foxglove—*Digitalis*. It was not in someone's old-fashioned garden, but was growing wild as it does in its native England and Scotland . . . As we drove down the Columbia, we saw more and more foxglove; this importation from the Old World is now very widespread throughout western Oregon and Washington. The fact that it will thrive on its own out here . . . is an indication of a rather English climate—moist, cool, with a relatively mild winter.—ROGER TORY PETERSON and JAMES FISHER, *Wild America*, 1955

FUME-ROOT. See CORYDALIS

G A R L I C—*Gar* is an archaic English word for a spear. Garlic, or *garleac,* means "spear leek." That is to say, a leek with spearlike leaves. The name for the garfish, with the long pointed snout, comes from the same source.

The ancients believed that garlic could effect the powers of a magnet, guard one against werewolves, sharpen the eyesight, and strengthen the body against fatigue. In *The Knights,* Aristophanes wrote: "Bolt down these cloves of garlic. Well primed with garlic you will have greater mettle for the fight." It was used in Chinese cooking as early as 2000 B.C. and was a popular ingredient in medieval European cooking, along with any other spicy or dominant flavor that could spruce up the taste of rancid food. Isaac Walton stuffed a pike with oysters and garlic, but concluded his recipe by saying that "the using of or not using of this Garlick is left to your discretion." In 1861, Mrs. Beeton's *Book of Household Management* mentioned garlic only once, in a chutney recipe. Otherwise, she dismissed it as having an "offensive smell, though French and Italian chefs considered it essential."

The wild garlics that grow throughout North America had long been known to the Indians as a powerful antiscorbutic. When Major Stephen Long explored Nebraska and Colorado in the 1820's, one hundred men in his party died of scurvy, to the confoundment of the expedition's physician. The Indians came forward with the green herbs and bulbs of a local wild garlic and cured the surviving victims. Ten years later, when Prince Maximilian of Wied was off on his two-year exploration of the Missouri River Valley, he too fell ill with scurvy and his case was considered hopeless. A Negro cook, who had been with Major Long, remembered the garlic cure and sent out a flock of Indian children to gather it for the prince. Maximilian ate the cut up bulbs and recovered.

The Indians also used bruised garlic buds to relieve the pain of bee and wasp stings and a poultice made from the ground stems to cure carbuncles.

> *Garlic.* A species of leek very much like that which appears in woods on hills in Sweden, grows at present on almost all sandy grain fields. The English here call it garlic. . . . When the cattle graze on such fields and eat the garlic, their milk, and the butter which is made of it, taste so strongly of it they are scarcely consumable. Sometimes they buy butter in the Philadelphia markets which tastes so strongly of garlic that it is useless.—PETER KALM, *Travels into North America*, 1748–1751

> We may divide women into two classes—those who use perfumeries, and those who do not. Others are content with any coarse scents, as citronella for the hair, cinnamon for the handkerchief, perhaps a sprig of peppermint or rosemary for Sunday to carry to church, and garlic—ugh!—for cooking. Such women exert little or no lasting fascination, and their husbands may be tempted to go outside of their own homes to find gratification. —ERNEST J. STEVENS, *Vital Sex and Love Facts*, 1923

> She smelled of garlic, and the sheets weren't very clean, and after it was all over when I was down on the street again, walking home, I thought that I never wanted to see her again.—E. HOWARD HUNT, *Stranger in Town*, 1946

> Garlick is the plant of the gods . . . —J. R. ANDERSON, *Garden Book*, 1768

GAYWINGS. See POLYGALA

GENTIAN, Pliny tells us, comes from Gentius, an Illyrian king, who first discovered the medicinal virtues of these plants and cured a mysterious fever which had stricken his army. And according to Hungarian legend, when the country was beset

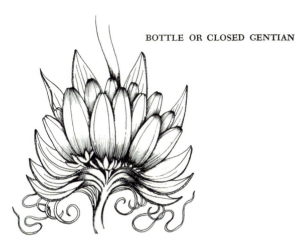

by plague in the eleventh century, Saint Ladislas, the king, went into the fields with bow and arrow and prayed that the arrow be directed to a plant that would save his people. He shot, and the arrow flew to the gentians, which Ladislas gathered, and wondrous cures were wrought. The root of the yellow European gentian, from which a liqueur also is made, is still used as a tonic and stomachic—medicinal uses which the American Indians found in many of our native gentians.

Of the dozen or so varieties in the United States, some are greenish, some white, but nevertheless the very sound of the word gentian says "blue." We have the bluest of purple blues in the closed, or bottle, gentians; the prairie gentians; the pine-barren gentians; and the ruff gentians of the west, where acres of them bloom in "gentian meadows." The fringed gentian, one of the most beautiful flowers in the world, is also one of the most elusive, because it's an annual and grows only from seed, not from last year's roots. The wind-scattered seeds often found a new, distant, secret colony, and not a trace will remain where the fringed gentian bloomed the year before.

My first fringed gentian was the reward of a forty-mile drive, taken one cold autumn day for the sole purpose of paying court

to its blue loveliness. . . . In bud the fringed petals are twisted one about the other. When the day is cloudy, or even, I should judge, if the wind is high, the full-blown flower closes in the same fashion. The individuals which grow in the shade are even more attractive than those which frequent to open. Their blue is lighter, with a silvery tinge which I do not recall in any other flower.
—FRANCES THEODORA PARSONS, *According to the Seasons*, 1902

Mr. Vick: I am a lover of flowers and a farmer's wife in a new country. We have here, on our prairies, a beautiful little gentian which you have surely missed in your travels, or you would have thought it worthy a place in your collection and any princely garden. The flower is nearly two inches long and an inch and a half across, being nearly in the shape of a bell, and of the richest and most intense blue imaginable. I call it October Beauty, because it blooms late in October when the prairie grass is brown and sere.
—Mrs. H.B.M., Vermillion, Kansas, *Vick's Magazine*, May, 1878

Down by the marsh, where the cows have trampled the bluish reed-grass, and the wild rose leaves are burning with dark purple-crimson, the bottle gentians are in bloom. Solemn flowers I find them, forever closed, forever in bud; mysterious because they will not appear until the sedge is a yellow ruin . . . and the great silence of the tenth month lies upon the desolate marsh . . . flowers with a sad dignity, offerings upon the grave of the year.
—DONALD CULROSS PEATTIE, *An Almanac for Moderns*, 1935

Fringed Gentian and Closed Gentian: These flowers, standing so erect upon their stems, might form veritable funnels to catch the dew and rain, but, to keep their pollen dry, the fringed gentian closes in cloudy or wet weather, and the closed gentian never opens at all. For this reason it has been thought that the latter flower was self-fertilized—a thing most unlikely on account of the positions and the successive maturing of the stamens and pistils. The colour, too, shows that this gentian strives to attract bees who alight upon it and tear apart the petals, as we would force our hands into a closed bag of peanuts. I have had the pleasure of seeing a bumblebee thus enter a closed gentian with an assurance that proved he was an old burglar, experienced in "breaking and taking."—HERBERT W. FAULKNER, *The Mysteries of the Flowers*, 1917

G E R A N I U M, and I am speaking of the true geraniums native to America, Europe, North Africa, and Japan—single, five-petaled, symmetrical flowers that range in color from pink to lavender to purple and blue. The name was originally Greek, *geranion*, which comes from *geranos*, or crane, because the seed vessels of these plants are pointed, like the bill of a crane. The common English nickname, quite logically, is cranesbill.

In the folklore of Islam, geraniums were said to be a gift from Allah. As the legend goes, Mahomet went in bathing one hot dusty day, leaving his shirt on a clump of weeds. When the prophet came out of the stream and picked up the shirt, the weeds had been transformed into geraniums.

The hothouse and window-box "geraniums" are another cup of tea altogether. They are principally of South African origin and belong to the genus *pelargonium,* or storksbill. Pelargos is Greek for stork, and again the name is descriptive of the beaked seed vessels. The storkbills were erroneously classified with the geraniums upon their introduction to Europe early in the 1700's. Although Linnaeus later classified the storkbilled "geraniums" into their own genus and gave them the botanic designation of *pelargonium,* the mix-up in names is still with us.

Our native geraniums, or cranesbills—pale lavender flowers with pink-veined petals—were used by the Indians, and later by the settlers, for a wide variety of ailments: cholera, gonorrhea, neuralgia, toothaches, and particularly as a styptic for open wounds.

June 19, 1852. Buttercups and geraniums cover the meadows, the latter appearing to float on the grass. It has lasted long, this rather tender flower.—HENRY DAVID THOREAU, *Journals*

In the cranesbill the mechanism of its seed pod may be likened to the catapult of antiquity, that is, the sudden release of a compressed spring. The full powers of this tiny catapult of the cranes-

bill have never been appreciated . . . but it is only comparatively recently, when walking in the midst of a retreat in the park, that I became fully aware of their energy. It was a still, sultry day in June, which so increased the hygrometric tension of the fast-ripening pistils. . . . They were quivering right and left. Occasionally a stray missile would strike my face or hand. Altogether the cranesbills were having a time of it; their volleys kept up an incessant bombardment. Curious to investigate the matter further, I picked a large number of the fruiting stems and carried them home for experiment. . . . The white cloths spread upon the floor were soon peppered to the distance of ten feet, and observing that many of the seeds fell from a rebound against the end wall and the ceiling, I opened up the passage-way and a few hours later here discovered a half-dozen of the black seeds over thirty feet away from their original position. It is hardly improbable that one of them more ambitious than the rest succeeded in reaching the open window and made the jump into my grass-plot.
—WILLIAM HAMILTON GIBSON, *Happy Hunting-grounds*, 1886

GILL-OVER-THE-GROUND, or ground ivy, originally a European plant, took off in all directions centuries ago, racing from continent to continent, and now grows wild in China and Japan and America. It is a member of the mint family and has tiny purple hooded flowers. There is some disagreement about the meaning of its name. Gill-over-the-ground is thought of by some lexicographers as a nickname like black-eyed susan or johnny-jump-up, because Gill or Jill is short for Gillian and was an old-fashioned word for a sweetheart—"Every Jack must have his Jill." Other authorities take the word gill to be a variation of the French verb *guiller,* to ferment, because leaves from this little trailing plant were used to flavor beer and ale before hops became the standard ingredient. And because of its use in brewing, the Anglo-Saxons called this plant alehoof, a name you will still run across occasionally, which simply means "ale ivy." It was widely used in medicines and tisanes, as well, and at one time in America was recommended as a cure for lead poisoning from paint.

As for flower lovers, their opinions are mixed. Some are charmed by gill-over-the ground, some are not. (I am.)

. . . the humble and obstreperous little creeping mint which is a pest in damp lawns rather than a plant to be introduced into an herb-garden. . . . The whole plant has a strong disagreeable odor.—MINNIE WATSON KAMM, *Old-Time Herbs*, 1939

As the pleasant aroma of its leaves suggests, this little plant is closely allied to catnip. Its common title of gill-over-the-ground appeals to one who is sufficiently without interest in pasture-land (for it is obnoxious to cattle) to appreciate the pleasant fashion in which this little immigrant has made itself at home here, brightening the earth with such a generous profusion of blossoms every May.—MRS. WILLIAM STARR DANA, *How to Know the Wild Flowers*, 1893

This is the little plant that the English love so dearly and which blooms abundantly in the pasturage every springtime. We have hardly the same fondness for it here and rather resent the calm manner in which it has taken possession of the soil.—ALICE LOUNSBERRY, *A Guide to the Wild Flowers*, 1899

Gill-over-the-ground is a rampant, spreading herb, but some cold dark north corner may need just what its trailing stems, shining crenulate leaves, and blue flowers may give us. Hyacinth and yellow "daffys" are enchanting planted in their midst.—HELEN NOYES WEBSTER, *Herbs*, 1939

G I N G E R was originally a Sanskrit word, *srngaverem*, which meant "horn body," a description of the root. *Srnga*, horn, and *vera*, body. The word was picked up by the Greeks as *zingiberis*, by the Romans as *gingiber*, by the French as *gingembre*, and finally emerged in English as ginger. This, of course, referred to the Indian ginger that has been cultivated since time immemorial and used in aromatic oils and in medicines, especially as a stimulant, and in cooking, either as a condiment or candied.

Wild ginger—another family but with the same taste—grows throughout the United States and the West Indies. John Gerard,

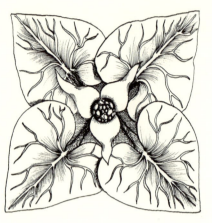

WILD GINGER

in 1597, wrote: "Our men which sacked Domingo in the Indies, digged it up there in sundry places wilde." Among the American Indians, native ginger was another of the esteemed medical herbs, and in twentieth century research, the roots were discovered to contain antibiotic substances which are "very active against Gram-positive pus-forming bacteria."

July 18, 1806 . . . One of the hunters in attempting to mount his horse, after shooting a deer, fell on a small piece of timber, which ran nearly two inches into the muscular part of his thigh. . . . The gentlest and strongest horse was therefore selected, and a sort of litter framed in such a manner as to enable the sick man to lie nearly at full length. . . . Soon after they passed another Indian fort on an island, and after making nine miles, halted to let the horses graze, and sent out a hunter to look for timber to make a canoe, and procure, if possible, some wild genger to make a poultice for Gibson's thigh, which was now exceedingly painful. —MERIWETHER LEWIS, *The Lewis and Clark Expedition,* 1804–1806

In the spring a warm hue comes among these closely-folded leaves, and presently a curious dull-colored bud begins to protrude its long tip from their midst. We soon see that its blunt appearance is due to the fact that the long prongs of he sepals are neatly folded in upon themselves, like the jointed legs of an insect. It must require considerable force in the flower to unfurl them. When at length expanded, these blossoms have the look of some rapacious, hobgoblin spider, lurking for its prey.—MARY ELIZABETH PARSONS, *Wild Flowers of California*, 1900

Wild ginger is another savage invader. Why the hills about us are not all carpeted with wild ginger is a deep mystery. Three small plants which we set out fifteen years ago have each spread over square yards; one of them reached down through a stone wall and reappeared rods away from its base of operations. We like wild ginger. Its rusty hidden flower makes a lovely design, though you have to stoop to see it . . . and it blooms, in its modest way, almost as early as bloodroot and arbutus. But enough is enough. For years now we have been weeding wild ginger and trying to give it away to friends who complain that nothing will grow in their dry soil.—LEWIS GANNETT, *Cream Hill*, 1949

G I N S E N G has been known to the Chinese for thousands of years as "the dose of immortality"—as an aphrodisiac, a restorer of youth and health, and a prolonger of life. The Asian species, which grew only in the mountains of Tartary and was worth its weight in silver, was known in Chinese as *jen-shen*, the "man-plant"—that is to say, a plant in the image of man, because the forked roots resembled the legs and torso of the human figure.

When French Jesuit missionaries in China reported on the medical and monetary value of ginseng, their descriptions of the plant were recognized by French botanists as a plant known to exist in the New World. The message was passed on to French Jesuits in Canada, and in 1716 North American ginseng was gathered near Montreal and shipped to France for re-sale to China. With that, the rush was on. The ginseng trade was an instant money-maker. In 1752, when a trader among the Mohawks "sent word to the Indians to gather as many roots as they could, as he expected to be there in 10 days to purchase them," the Moravian missionaries at Onondago took to the woods themselves "to gather roots, in order to buy several blankets, as the nights were growing cold." By the end of the 1700's, the root was bringing up to a dollar a pound in Virginia. It was a prime cargo in the early days of the U.S. clipper ships on the China run, and fortunes were made. Another ginseng rush early in the 1900's nearly eradicated the plant, and today it can be found only in isolated places. The ginseng now sold among the teas and vitamins in health food stores is usually an import, via Korea.

The Indians had always been aware of ginseng, using it for fevers, headaches, coughs, nausea, and a strengthener of mental powers, but in 1810 Dr. Benjamin Smith Barton of Philadelphia wrote that they did not "so highly esteem the Ginseng as their Tartar brethren in Asia do." There was no aphrodisiacal mystique or reverence surrounding the plant, as in the Orient, but an Indian name for it, like the Chinese, compared ginseng to the human anatomy.

> *Quebec. August, 1749.* The Iroquois call the ginseng roots *Garangtoging,* which is said signifies a child, the roots bearing a faint resemblance to one; but others are of the opinion that they mean the thigh and leg by it, and the roots look very much like that. . . . During my stay in Canada all the merchants at Quebec and Montreal received orders from their correspondents in France. . . . The Indians especially travelled about the country to collect as much as they could. The Indians in the neighborhood of this town were likewise so much taken up with this business that the French farmers were not able during that to hire a single Indian, as they commonly do to help them in the harvest.—PETER KALM, *Travels into North America,* 1748–1751

> As a help to bear Fatigue I used to chew a Root of Ginseng as I walk't along. This kept up my Spirits, and made me trip away as nimbly in my Jack-Boots as younger men could in their Shoes. This plant is in high esteem in China. . . . It grows also on the northern continent of America, near the Mountains, but as sparingly as Truth & Public Spirit. . . . Its vertues are, that it gives an uncommon Warmth and Vigour to the Blood, and frisks the Spirits. It chears the Heart even of a Man that has a bad Wife. . . . It helps the Memory, and would quicken even Helvetian dullness. In one word, it will make a Man live a great while,

and very well while he does live. . . . However, tis of little use in the Feats of Love, as a great prince once found, who hearing of its invigorating Quality, sent as far as China for some of it, though his ladys could not boast of any Advantage thereby.—WILLIAM BYRD, *Histories of the Dividing Line Betwixt Virginia and North Carolina,* 1728

When ginseng was discovered in North America, the herbalists of the Flowery Kingdom, anxious to have it, offered high prices. Both the Cherokees and the mountain folk ranged widely over the hills in their assiduous search for the precious "sang." A mountaineer once described to Donald Culross Peattie a group of "sang diggers": *They was the most terrifying people I ever see. I was over in the balsams, when I see them coming through the woods—men and women with eyes that didn't seem to see nothing, and their clothes all in tatters, and their hair all lank and falling down on their shoulders. They humped along through the woods like b'ars, muttering to themselves all the time, and stooping, and digging, and cursing and humping on and digging again.*—ROGER TOREY PETERSON and JAMES FISHER, *Wild America,* 1955

GLOBE LILY, or GLOBE TULIP. See MARIPOSA

GOLDEN RAGWORT. See GROUNDSEL

GRASS-PINK. See CALOPOGON

GROUND IVY. See GILL-OVER-THE-GROUND

GROUNDSEL—We have both the European and the American groundsels growing wild. By and large, they are unprepossessing plants with raggedy leaves, typical of the ragwort family to which they belong, and their small yellow flowers go to seed with downy heads—like the dandelion. The most prevalent American variety has larger, brighter, aster-like flowers and is generally known as golden ragwort. Squaw weed is another old nickname, because it was used among the Indians as a remedy for female complaints and to ease the pains of childbirth. But above all, it was particularly prized by the Indians as an unguent for wounds and as a hemostatic.

Ancient Greek and Arabian physicans had discovered the same healing properties in the European plants, and a poultice of groundsel, mixed with a fine powder of frankincense, was used over the centuries to draw wounds and abcesses. Because of its healing powers, the Anglo-Saxons gave the plant the name *gundeswelge,* the "pus-swallower," from *gund,* pus, and *swelgan,* to swallow. The Anglo-Saxon was gradually modified in Middle English to *grundswilie,* and from there to *grunsel,* and finally to groundsel.

> *August,* 1803. We saw before us the hills of Loch Lomond, Ben Lomond, and another, distinct each by itself. . . . Travelled for some miles along the open country, which was all without hedgerows, sometimes arable, sometimes moorish, and often whole tracts covered with grunsel. There was one field, which one might have believed had been sown with grunsel, it was so regularly covered with it; contiguous to it were other fields of the same size and shape, one of clover, one of potatoes, all equally regular crops. The oddness of this appearance, the grunsel being uncommonly luxuriant, and the field as yellow as gold, made William laugh. C. [Samuel Taylor Coleridge] was melancholy upon it, observing that there was land enough wasted to rear a healthy child.—DOROTHY WORDSWORTH, *Recollections of a Tour Made in Scotland*

HAREBELL—This entry is less of a definition and more of a spelling lesson. The name is not hairbell, but harebell —and has always been so.

HAREBELL

A curt no-nonsense explanation of this mix-up was given by the Reverend Walter Skeat in his *Etymological Dictionary of the English Language,* 1881. "HAREBELL . . . has been supposed to be a corruption of *hair-bell,* with reference to the slenderness of the stalk. The apparent absence of reason for the name is, however, in favour of the etymology from *hare,* as will be seen by consulting the fanciful AS. names of plants given in Cockayne's *Leechdoms.* To name plants from animals was the old custom; hence hare's beard, hare's ear, hare's foot, hare's lettuce, hare's palace, hare's tail. . . . The spelling of *hair-bell* savours of modern science, but certainly not of the principles of English etymology."

The harebell, a flower of cold crisp climates, is native to North America, Europe, and Asia. Once upon a time in Scotland these flowers were also called witches' thimbles, an interesting link with the name harebell, because witches were said to transform themselves into hares. Therefore, it was bad luck to have a hare cross your path, and northern fishermen in the British Isles would not go out in their boats if they met a hare on their way to the harbor. And in keeping with the witch-hare legends, hare meat was said to be a "black" meat that bred melancholy and incubi and fearful dreams.

Glenora Peak. The harebell appears at about four thousand feet and extends to the summit, dwarfing in stature but maintaining the size of its handsome bells until they seem to be lieing loose and detached on the ground as if like snow flowers they had fallen from the sky; and, though frail and delicate-looking, none of its companions is more enduring or rings out the praise of beauty-loving Nature in tones more appreciable to mortals.—JOHN MUIR, *Travels in Alaska,* 1915

H A W K W E E D—The name comes from European folk-lore, where it was said that hawks sharpened their eyesight with juice from these plants. There are a number of American hawk-weeds with yellow-daisy-like flowers, but the two handsomest varieties were introduced from the Old World—the bright orange-crimson hawkweed and the yellow hawkweed. These were originally brought to England from the continent and were known in the early days as French lungwort because of their use in curing pulminary ailments. The orange variety was also nicknamed Grim the Collier. In his *Herbal,* 1597, Gerard explained why: "The stalkes and cups of the floures are all set thicke with a blackish downe or hairinesse as if it were the dust of coals; whence the women, who keep it in their gardens for novelties sake, have named it Grim the Collier. . . . This is a stranger and only to be found in some few gardens." Both of these strangers, the yellow and the orange, now blaze in American meadows, beautiful to the eye, but a pest to farmers as they were in the Old World, where they got the nicknames we still use today: devil's-bit, king devil, and devil's-paintbrush.

The oaks cast broad shadows on the short velvety sward, not so sharp and definite as those of June, but tender, and, as it were, drawn with a loving hand. They were large shadows, though it was mid-day—a sign that the sun was no longer at his greatest height, but declining. Pleasant as it was, there was regret in the thought that the summer was going fast. Another sign—the grass by the gateway, an acre of it, was brightly yellow with hawkweeds. —ROBERT JEFFRIES, 1848–1887, *The Open Air*

84

I was walking through an August meadow when I saw, on a little knoll, a bit of most vivid orange, verging on a crimson. I knew of no flower of such a complexion frequenting such a place as that. On investigation, it proved to be a stranger. It had a rough, hairy, leafless stem about a foot high, surmounted by a corymbose cluster of flowers of dark vivid orange color. The leaves were deeply notched and toothed, very bristly, and were pressed flat to the ground. The whole plant was a veritable Esau for hairs, and it seemed to lay upon the ground as if it was not going to let go easily. And what a fiery plume it had! . . . The plant seemed to be a species of hawkweed . . . but I could not find it mentioned in our botanies.

A few days later, on the edge of an adjoining county ten miles distant, I found, probably, its headquarters. It had appeared there a few years before and was thought to have escaped from some farmer's dooryard. Patches of it were appearing here and there in the fields. . . . Its seeds are winged like those of the dandelions, and it sows itself far and near.—JOHN BURROUGHS, *Riverby*, 1894

H E A T H and H E A T H E R—In their original sense, heath and heather meant a plant that grew on a heath, and heath comes from the Anglo-Saxon *haeth,* a wasteland. This is also the root word for heathen—that is, people living in a wilderness or wasteland, removed from the salvation of the Church.

Nowadays, heather has generally come to mean Scotch heather, the bonny purple heather of the highlands, though it also grows throughout moorlands in Europe and Asia Minor. This common heather is now an American plant, too, naturalized from overseas and growing wild from Newfoundland to Michigan, and southward to the mountains of West Virginia. It was the all-purpose plant to the Scots—fodder for cattle, food for the red grouse, thatch for roofing, honey for the bees, baskets from the woven roots, brooms from the twigs, and mats of heather, blossom side up, for bedding.

The word heath has generally come to mean the worldwide family of plants that includes such North American varieties as blueberries, cranberries, wintergreens, trailing arbutus, azaleas, and rhododendrons. In the following quotation, John Muir speaks of *Cassiope,* a western heath named for Andromeda's mother, early in the 1800's, by David Don, an English botanist who followed Linnaeus' earlier tradition of classical allusions. Muir also speaks of *Bryanthus,* named by Don's brother George Don; it means "moss-flower," from the Greek *bryon,* moss, and *anthus,* flower. But despite their Grecian titles, both of these flowering plants are known locally, with no further ado, as "mountain heather."

The glory of the alpine regions are the heathworts. . . . The lowly, hardy, adventurous cassiope has exceedingly slender creeping branches, scalelike leaves, and pale pink or white waxen bell flowers. In July it spreads a wavering, interrupted belt of the loveliest bloom around glacier lakes and meadows and across wild moory expanses, between roaring streams, all along the Sierra, and northward beneath cold skies by way of the mountain chains to the Arctic regions . . .

Bryanthus, the companion of cassiope, accompanies it as far north as southeastern Alaska, where together they weave thick plushy beds on rounded mountain tops above the glaciers. . . . The wide bell-shaped flowers are bright purple, about three-fourths of an inch in diameter, hundreds to the square yard. . . . No Highlander in heather enjoys a more luxurious rest than the Sierra mountaineer in a bed of blooming bryanthus. And imagine the show on calm dewy mornings, when there is a radiant globe in the throat of every flower, and smaller gems on the needle-shaped leaves, the sunbeams pouring through them.—JOHN MUIR, *Our National Parks,* 1901

Most attractive is the Heather with its pink and white flowers raceming every shoot and recalling Scotland and other parts of Europe. These plants of nest-like habit are of strong social instinct —clannish to the extreme. They strive to cover the land in a carpet of growth, loving the sunshine and wind, resenting the presence of other plants and sulking bitterly when tall bushes invade their domain.—E. H. WILSON, *America's Greatest Garden, the Arnold Arboretum,* 1925

HENBANE. See under BANE

HEPATICA is from the Greek *hepar*, or liver, which is the root word, of course, for hepatitis and all other liver-associated medical terms. In ancient days, when doctors and theologians labored under the belief that God indicated, in some fashion, the uses to which His creations could be put by man, the leaves of this plant—through a curious stretch of the imagination—were thought to resemble the lobes of the liver. Hence, its name and its use as a remedy for liver ailments. By extension, common English nicknames are liver-leaf and liverwort—not to be confused with the primitive, non-flowering liverworts that are related to the mosses.

The American Indians, however, did not see the liver in the leaves of our native hepaticas. They used the plants to cure vertigo, crosseyes, and coughs.

February 14, 1802. The sun shines out, but it has been a hard frost in the night. There are some little snowdrops that are afraid to put their white heads quite out, and a few blossoms of hepatica that are half-starved.—DOROTHY WORDSWORTH, *Journal*

HEPATICA

There are many things left for May, but nothing fairer, if as fair, as the first flower, the hepatica. I find I have never admired this little firstling half enough. When at the maturity of its charms, it is certainly the gem of the woods. What an individuality it has! No two clusters are alike; all shades and sizes; some are snow-white, some pale pink, with just a tinge of violet, some deep purple, others the purest blue, others blue touched with lilac. A solitary blue-purple one, fully expanded and rising over the brown leaves or the green moss, its cluster of minute anthers showing like a group of pale stars on its little firmament. . . .

Then, there are individual hepaticas, or individual families among them, that are sweet-scented. The gift seems as capricious as the gift of genius in families. You cannot tell which the fragrant ones are till you try them. Sometimes it is the large white ones, sometimes the large purple ones, sometimes the small pink ones. The odor is faint, and recalls that of the sweet violets.—JOHN BURROUGHS, *Signs and Seasons*, 1892

HERB-ROBERT, one of the cranesbills, or true geraniums, came to us from Europe. It's a cold climate plant that grows as far north as the Arctic circle and has a strong scented resinous secretion. Peter Kalm (the Swedish naturalist who visited America in the 1750's) compared the scent of skunk to that of herb-robert, for the edification of his European readers who had never seen, much less smelled, an American skunk. Because of the plant's pungent odor, one of its old names was dragon's blood, and because of its ruddy stem, the Scots called it red shanks. In rural England, where it was thought to bring immediate and dire misfortune to those who picked it, death-come-quickly was another familiar name. But herb-robert was indeed picked and widely used for curing wounds and ulcers and for staunching blood.

Some say the name was given in honor of Rupert, patron saint of Bavaria; others, that it honors the Benedictine monk, St. Robert, who died in 1067 and cured a plague through the beneficence of this plant. Still others assert that it honors Robert, Duke of Normandy, the son of William the Conqueror, whose name was also associated with medicine. On his way home from the Crusades, Robert stopped at the hospital in Salerno with a wound that had degenerated into a fistulous ulcer. The Salerno physicians cured him, and as a tribute to the Duke's royal patronage, they compiled a medical book that remained the standard text for several centuries.

It sometimes makes its uninvited appearance in my rock garden and is so pretty and altogether amusing that I let it stay. Then presently I awake to the fact that my small area is positively overrun with Herb Robert and with the safety of choice treasures in mind it must be rooted out. It is a horrid task, for when bruised or broken it fills the world with expostulations in the form of a nasty odor which clings to clothing and hands for a long time.
—LOUISE BEEBE WILDER, *The Fragrant Path*, 1932

Spring proper, bearer of many suspect scents, the sum total of which is calculated to enchant us. . . . That is why I retire to my modest lair, along paths embroidered perchance by the wild geranium, known as Herb-Robert, with its insignificant flowers and seeds the shape of a crane's bill. If by accident you happen to brush your fingers against it they will retain a sharp fragrance, a little too keen to be agreeable. I myself take pleasure in crushing its purplish stem and leaves, for this sets me dreaming . . .
—COLETTE, *For a Flower Album*, 1949

H Y A C I N T H—The true hyacinths of the Mediterranean region are pale blue field flowers that became the forebears of our lush garden varieties, first developed by the Dutch in the 1700's. But the name is a catchy one, and it has been given to any number of other flowers that have no direct claim to the hyacinth pedigree.

Our blue and white camass is often called wild hyacinth. We have an insidious but incredibly beautiful water weed from South America that was introduced at the New Orleans Cotton Exposition in 1884 and is now known to all of us as the water hyacinth. On the west coat, a native lily is nicknamed twining hyacinth, and one of our new arrivals, now listed in wildflower guides, is the little many-belled, royal blue "grape hyacinth," originally a garden import from the Caucasus, Turkey, and the Mediterranean shores. Ruskin described their scent as the distillation of "a cluster of grapes and a hive of honey."

Hyacinth is a Greek word of no known meaning. The first of the flowers with this name were said to have sprung from the blood of Hyacinthus, a Greek youth thus immortalized by Apollo.

Mercury: The amiable Hyacinthus is dead? I should like to know how it happened.

Apollo: He was learning by practice to throw the discus, and I was his companion. . . . When I threw the discus, as we had many time before, high up in the air, this cursed Zephyr gave a blast downwards and drove it falling with such force against the boy's head, that the blood gushed in torrents from the wound, and the boy died on the spot. From his blood, I caused the earth to produce the fairest and loveliest of all flowers. . . . Have I not reason to be melancholy?

Mercury: No. Since you knew you had chosen a mortal for your favourite, how can you take it amiss that he is dead?—Lucian of Samosata, *Dialogues*, Second Century, A.D.

Of all the pretty flowers that abound in California, we know of nothing prettier than the twining Hyacinth. The flowers are a very fine pink, or deep rose. It grows in the mountains, and twines over every bush it can reach. After it gets to the top of the bush, it lets go of the earth and goes on blooming and seeding for weeks and months, regardless of the burning sun by day or the cool mountain air by night. . . . People often bring the stem indoors and allow it to climb up over the curtains.—*Vick's Magazine*, May, 1878

Blue is a lovely and beloved color at any season in the garden, but in the spring it is verily, the salt in the broth. Now let us see what is at hand. Happily the spring is wealthy in blue flowers, though they largely do not spring from our own soil. Violets can by no stretch of the imagination be called blue. In our own spacious wild we have the Hepatica, blue enough at times, though more often white or pale purple, the little Quaker Lady that sweeps the spring meadows with pale blue frost, the Virginia

Cowslip. . . . But from foreign parts we derive a number of little blue-flowered bulbs. The Grape Hyacinth has naturalized itself in certain neighborhoods, and a delightful surprise it is to find this pretty alien holding its own in the rough grass of meadow and roadside. Do not admit them to your rock garden (they are too "spreadacious," as a friend says), but give them the freedom of your banks and braes and shrubbery borders.—LOUISE BEEBE WILDER, *What Happens in My Garden*, 1935

In the Everglades. The rivers which we crossed were like botanical gardens. White spider lilies raised their pallid blooms at the edges of dark bogs, and once in an open spot we saw the golden trumpet of a carnivorous plant related to the pitcher plant. Every stream, every water-filled ditch, was choked with water hyacinths, their orchid-like blossoms forming masses of lavender bloom on the sluggish water. Buoyed up by bladders at the bases of their bright green leaves they slowly drifted on the current, like miniature floating gardens. No one will deny that this alien from Brazil is beautiful, but its beauty is almost the kiss of death to a southern stream. It soon crowds out the native aquatic plants. This would be forgivable if birds and other wild creatures found it edible, but they do not, although cows will often wade up to their bellies to eat it. This pest seems to divide, subdivide and multiply like the amoeba. . . . One Floridian tossed some plants from her fish pool into the St. Johns River; within ten years, they had multiplied some millions of times, had traveled many miles and completely choked the broad river in places. Since then, staggering amounts—millions of dollars—have been appropriated to keep the St. Johns and other hyacinth-infested water navigable. —ROGER TORY PETERSON and JAMES FISHER, *Wild America*, 1955

IMPATIENCE. See TOUCH-ME-NOT

INDIAN SHOT. See CANNA

INDIAN TOBACCO. See under LOBELIA

I R I S—She was the goddess of the rainbow and a member of Juno's court, where her special office was to receive the souls of dying women. Moreover, Iris was a model of every virtue and so impressed Juno with her purity (she resisted Jupiter's blandishments), that Juno decided to commemorate her forever with a flower that would bear Iris' name and bloom in the rainbow colors of Iris' robes.

Iris were cultivated in ancient Japan, Babylonia, and Egypt. Saracen armies carried white iris with them to plant on the graves of their dead. Clovis, king of the Franks, chose iris as his symbol when his army safely forded a river where the shallow water bloomed with wild iris. Louis VII, home from the second crusade, chose iris as his victory symbol for the royal coat-of-arms—the *fleur-de-Louis,* or *fleur-de-lys.* In Japan and Europe, the roots were ground for face powders, sachet-powders, and perfumes, and in America the Indians used the highly cathartic roots of the native blue iris in medicines.

The nickname "flag" means exactly that—a flag, from the Middle English *flakken,* to flutter, because the plant flutters in the wind. Flag was a general term for any reed or rush, and is still sometimes used in that sense. The verb to flag, to grow weary, comes from the same source—to flutter, in other words, to lose strength. (In case you're concerned about flagstone, that comes from a Nordic root, *flaga,* a slab or slice of sod or stone.)

Albany, New York. October 30, 1749. The Indians make use of the iris root as a remedy for sores on the legs. This cure is prepared as follows. They take the root, wash it clean, boil it a little, then crush it between a couple of stones. They spread this crushed root as a poultice over the sores and at the same time rub the leg with the water in which the root is boiled. Colonel Lydius said that he had seen great cures brought about by the use of this remedy. It is the blue Iris, which is extremely common here . . .
—PETER KALM, *Travels into North America,* 1748–1751

92

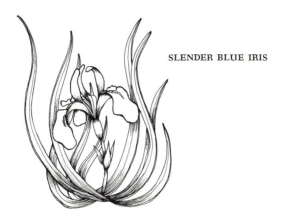

Georgia. December, 1777. An Ottasses Indian village. At this time the town was fasting, taking medicine, and I think I may say praying, to avert a grievous calamity of sickness which had lately afflicted them and laid in the grave abundance of their citizens. They fast seven or eight days, during which time they eat or drink nothing but a meager gruel made of a little corn flour and water; taking at the same time, by way of medicine or physic, a strong decoction of the roots of the Iris versicolor, which is a powerful cathartic. They hold this root in high estimation; every town cultivates a little plantation of it, having a large artificial pond, just without the pond, planted and almost overgrown with it . . . —WILLIAM BARTRAM, *Travels,* 1773–1778

Concord, Massachusetts. June 12, 1852. The blue flag, notwithstanding its rich furniture, its fringed, re-curved parasols over its anthers, and its variously streaked and colored petals, is loose and coarse in its habit. How completely all character is expressed by flowers. This is a little too showy and gaudy, like some women's bonnets. Yet it belongs to the meadow and ornaments it much. —HENRY DAVID THOREAU, *Journals*

Mandarin, Florida. March, 1872. It was a most heavenly morning. . . . In the low swamp-land near our home is a perfect field of blue iris, whose bending leaves were all beaded with dew; and we walked in among them, admiring the wonderful vividness of their coloring, and gathering the choicest to fill a large vase. . . .

The blue St. John's lay in misty bands of light and shade in the distance; and the mocking-birds and red-birds were singing a loud *Te Deum.*—HARRIET BEECHER STOWE, *Palmetto-Leaves,* 1873

J A C K - I N - T H E - P U L P I T. See under ARUM

J A C O B 'S - L A D D E R. See under VALERIAN

J E W E L W E E D. See TOUCH-ME-NOT

J I M S O N W E E D, with blue or white trumpet-shaped flowers and prickly fruit, is a member of the nightshade family. The name is a corruption of Jamestown weed, which was given to the plant in colonial days because it first grew wild in America in and around Jamestown, Virginia. Presumably it had been brought from England as a medicinal plant. Boiled with hog's grease, Jimsonweed made a healing unguent for burns from "fire, water, boiling lead, gunpowder, and lightning."

The narcotic powers of Jimsonweed had been known in the Old World since the beginning of recorded history, and its scientific name, *Datura,* is from its ancient Hindu name, *Dhatura.* In the Orient it was said that goats who had eaten the plant would manifest strange behaviors and try to walk on their hind feet like men. Some scholars have suggested that this may have been the drug inhaled by the Delphic oracles, who mumbled their prophesies while seated on a gold tripod over a chasm that emitted mysterious, narcotic vapors. As an hallucinogen, it is still being experimented with today.

There is another variety native to South America that was known as the thorn apple of Peru upon its introduction to Europe

94

JIMSONWEED

by the Spanish. Both the Asiatic and South American Jimson-weeds are now common across the United States. Thorn-apple has become a nickname for both varieties, and so has devil's-trumpet.

This, being an early plant, was gathered very young for a boiled salad, by some of the soldiers sent thither to quell the rebellion of Bacon [1676]; and some of them ate plentifully of it, the effect of which was a very pleasant comedy, for they turned natural fools upon it for several days: one would blow up a feather in the air; another would dart straws at it with much fury; and another, stark naked, was sitting up in a corner like a monkey, grinning and making mows [grimaces] at them; a fourth would fondly kiss and paw his companions, and sneer in their faces, with a countenance more antic than any in a Dutch droll. In this frantic condition they were confined, lest they should, in their folly, destroy themselves—though it was observed that all their actions were full of innocence and good nature. Indeed, they were not very cleanly. A thousand such simple tricks they played, and after eleven days returned to themselves again, not remembering anything that had passed.—ROBERT BEVERLY, *History of the Present State of Virginia*, 1705

Thomas Jefferson wrote the following letter to a friend who had sent him a new poisonous botanic specimen from the southwest, with the idea that Jefferson might want to add it to his collection in the Monticello gardens. You will see Jefferson's reasons for not planting it. The Marquis de Condorcet, who is mentioned in this letter, was a mathematician and philosopher condemned during the French Revolution.

. . . I have so many grandchildren and others who might be endangered by the poison plant, that I think the risk overbalances the curiosity of trying it. The most elegant thing of that kind known is a preparation of the Jamestown weed. Datura-Stramonium, invented by French in the time of Robespierre. Every man of firmness carried it constantly in his pocket to anticipate the guillotine. It brings on the sleep of death as quietly as fatigue does the ordinary sleep, without the least struggle or motion. Condorcet, who had recourse to it, was found lifeless on his bed a few minutes after his landlady had left him there, and even the slipper which she had observed half suspended on his foot was not shaken off.—THOMAS JEFFERSON, Monticello, July 14, 1813

JOE-PYE WEED—A purely American plant and, like its cousin boneset, a tall handsome, end-of-the-summer flower that is most at home in wet thickets. The Indians used it as a medicine for fevers and kidney complaints, and the early names given this plant by colonial settlers were ague weed, Indian sage, kidney-root, and gravel-root (because it was said to dissolve kidney stones).

The morning mists of late August swirl and eddy, and the shades of the old herb doctors may be there, especially of Joe Pye, who would be appraising the crop of wild herbs at the river's margin and back at the pasture's uncut fence line. His namesake plant . . . is in full blossom in the damp lowlands, magenta-red and unmistakable.

Joe Pye was an Indian known for his special skill as a "yarb man" who made the rounds of rural New England in the late 1700's. He apparently was specially skilled at reducing fevers. One of the few records of him show that he bought "1 qt rum,. 1s 6p" at a tavern in Stockbridge, Mass., in 1775, so perhaps he made an elixir as well as an herb infusion. In any case, he is the only herb doctor we know who had a plant named for him. Joe-Pye weed is still its common name.

So those eddying mists this morning could have been more than a swirl of vapor. If old Joe Pye's spirit was there, he must have been appraising the season's yield. . . . And almost certainly smiling his satisfaction at the abundance of his own special herb, the tall, magenta-flowered Joe-Pye weed.—*The New York Times*, August 29, 1971

KING DEVIL. See HAWKWEED

KNAPWEED—All told, there are some six hundred varieties in this family, most of them native to Europe and Eastern Asia. We have our own American varieties, but most of our wild knapweeds were introduced from overseas. They are usually late bloomers, along with goldenrods and asters, and the typical knapweed flower is pinkish-purple, tending to blue.

As a family, they have a surfeit of common names—star-thistle, ragged sailor, bluebottle, hardhead, cornflower, bachelor's button, caltrop, and centaury. Despite the efforts of purists to assign specific nicknames to specific varieties, they are very loosely used. One man's star thistle is another man's bluebottle.

But to begin at the beginning. Knapweed comes from the Old English and German *knobbe*—a knop or a knob, a bump, a button, a bud—and refers to the head of the flower which blooms from a hard compact bud and a compact, comparatively large bract, like the thistle, which is a near relative. Hence, the next nickname, star thistle. Bluebottle and hardhead are descriptive names, and so is ragged sailor, because of the raggedy petals. Cornflower was originally given to the pure blue species so common in European cornfields. (In Europe corn does not mean our

Indian corn, or maize; it means any sort of wheat or grain.)

Bachelor's button seems to have been given as a nickname because the buds resemble a kind of old-fashioned button made with a metal loop. The loop went through the button hole and was secured with a small metal bar. No sewing was required. Therefore, they were buttons for bachelors. (A similar kind is still used today for men's dress shirts and vests.) However, it has also been said that the flowers were used for love magic, that a girl who hid cornflowers, or knapweed, under her apron would win the bachelor of her choice through some sort of floral abracadabra.

The name caltrop (or caltrap or calthrop) is usually confined to the knapweed with long spines on the bract—very thistle-like. The name was borrowed in the middle ages from a weapon—a four-pointed iron object that was stuck into the ground, one spike projecting upward, to cripple the enemy's cavalry on the battle field. This iron object was a "foot trap," a *calcatrappa* in Medieval Latin, from *calcare,* to step or tread, and *trappa,* or trap. In English, *calcatrappa* was abbreviated to caltrop, and not only did caltrop refer to the spiked weapon, but also to the knapweed with the spiney bract. The French, too, have a variation on the original Latin—the word *chausse-trape,* which is used both for the weapon and the flower.

Now, centaury. Centaury, as a name for the various knapweeds, is a mistake. It happened this way. Chiron the centaur was accidentally but painfully wounded by Hercules' poisoned arrows. However, through the miraculous power of a certain kind of gentian, Chiron's wounds were healed. Thereafter, these particular gentians were known as *centauriums,* and still are. Around 288 B.C., a Greek philosopher, Theophrastus, wrote a history of plants in which he identified certain of the knapweeds as *Centaurea,* thus linking them with Chiron the centaur and his fabled medical knowledge. But knapweeds have no medical value whatsoever, unlike the gentians, which *do,* and could give rise to a fable about miraculous cures from poisoned arrows. At any rate,

Lucretius and Virgil both picked up Theophrastus' knapweed-*Centaurea*, and from there on the name stuck.

Both the ancient names are still with us today—*Centaurium*, for a kind of gentian, and *Centaurea*, for the genus to which knapweeds, cornflowers, bachelor's buttons, etc. all belong. To further add to the muddle, these particular gentians and the knapweeds are both nicknamed "centaury."

We have an American knapweed, *Centaurea americana*, which is often cultivated and goes by the nickname of basket-flower, because of the woven basket-like appearance of the bracts. This plant was discovered by Thomas Nuttall during his botanic wanderings early in the 1800's through the Mississippi and Missouri river valleys. Nuttall's name is usually associated with ornithology because he made his mark with a manual of American birds. Flowers, however, seem to have been his first and last love. Nuttall became curator of the Botanic Garden at Harvard, and upon inheriting an uncle's estate in Liverpool in 1842, he returned to England and devoted the rest of his life to the cultivation of rare plants. And in his English garden were many American species, often grown from seeds and specimens he had himself collected in the western travels of his youth. There is more about Thomas Nuttall under WISTERIA.

> *Centurea Americana* is confined in the United States to the dry regions of Texas, Arkansas, and the Indian Territory, where it has a singularly beautiful appearance, being often the only showy plant on the dry sterile soil, for the pretty ones are generally to be found only along the water courses, or where the ground may be moist. Still it has no objection to more favorable locations under other circumstances, as its luxurious growth and fine blossoms when under garden culture show. At least, this dry location is the experience of this writer, who collected it in northern Texas. . . . Our plant is of particular interest for its native beauty and its easy adaption.—THOMAS MEEHAN, *The Native Flowers and Ferns of the United States*, 1880

Next morning the August sun shone, and the wood was all

99

a-hum with insects . . . bumble-bees went wandering among the ferns in the copse and in the ditches and calling at every purple heath blossom and the purple knapweeds and purple thistles.
—RICHARD JEFFRIES, 1848–1887, *The Pine Wood*

LADIES'-TRESSES—A sweet-scented wild orchid with varieties native to America and Europe. Nowadays, the word tress has come to mean a curl or a lock of hair, but in its original meaning it was a braid, and ladies'-tresses is a descriptive nickname, because the white flowers spiral up the stem in a pattern resembling a braid or plait.

An earlier nickname that you'll often run across both in England and America is ladies'-traces instead of tresses, which caused a certain confusion among Victorian etymologists, because braided ropes used in horse harness and the braided straw used to tie up strings of onions were called traces, and so were the cords or laces used to tie a lady's bodice or corselette. There were any number of farfetched explanations for the flower's name. But both tress and trace come from the same root—the Latin *tricia,* or plait, which in turn comes from the Greek *tricha,* or three-fold, because plaits and braids are woven from three strands. A trace is a tress, and a tress is a trace. And there the matter ends.

Occasionally this plant becomes ambitious. Leaving the low, "wet places" to which it is assigned by the botanists, it climbs far up the hill-sides. I never remember seeing it in greater abundance or more fragrant and perfect than in a field high up on the Catskill Mountains. The mention or sight of this little orchid, instantly recalls that breezy upland with its far-reaching view, and its hum of eager bees, which were drinking the rare sweets of the late year from the myriad spires among which I rested on September morning.—FRANCES THEODORA PARSONS, *According to the Seasons,* 1902

LADY'S-SLIPPER—The name is of ancient vintage, given to the European varieties by medieval botanists in honor of the Virgin. The original Latin for lady's-slipper was *Calceolus marianus*—"the shoe of Mary." The old French names for these wild orchids were *sabot de la Vierge* and *soulier de Notre Dame*—the "Virgin's sabot," and "Our Lady's shoe." However, the medieval association with the Virgin was eventually put aside, perhaps because of the Reformation, and Venus became the lady in question. Linnaeus devised the scientific designation of *Cypripedium*, from the Greek *Kypris*, Venus, and *podion*, slipper or little foot, and in French, for example, a lady's-slipper was no longer the *sabot de la Vierge*, but became the *sabot de Venus*. Similarly, Venus'-slipper was a common nickname both in England and America until quite recently.

But nicknames are rife for this family of flowers—squirrel shoe, Noah's ark, old goose, camel's foot, silver slipper (for a rare white variety), and ram's head (for an even rarer species, small enough to fit in a thimble). Moccasin flower and whip-poor-will shoe are uniquely American nicknames.

Our Ladies Shoo or Slipper. . . . At the top of the stalke groweth one single floure, fashioned on the one side like an egg; on the other side it is open, empty, and hollow, and of the forme of a shoo or slipper; of a yellow colour on the outside, and of a shining deepe yellow on the inside. The middle part is compassed about with foure leaves of a bright purple colour, often of a light red or obscure crimson. . . . Ladies Slipper groweth upon the mountains of Germany, Hungary, and Poland. I have a plant thereof in my garden, which I received from Mr. Garret, Apothecary, my very good friend. It is also reported to grow in the North parts of this kingdome. . . . Touching the faculties of our Ladies Shoo we have nothing to write, it being not sufficiently known to the old Writers; no nor to the new.—JOHN GERARD, *Herbal*, 1597

Report came to me that in a certain quaking sphagnum bog in the woods the showy lady's-slipper could be found. The locality proved to be the marrowy grave of an extinct lake or black tarn. On the borders of it the white azalea was in bloom, fast fading.

YELLOW LADY'S-SLIPPER

In the midst of it were spruces and black ash and giant ferns and, low in the spongy, mossy bottom, the pitcher plant. The lady's-slipper grew in little groups and companies all about. Never have I beheld a prettier sight—so gray, so festive, so holiday looking. Were they so many gay bonnets rising above the foliage? or were they flocks of white doves with purple-stained breasts just lifting up their wings to take flight? or were they little fleets of fairy boats, with sail set, tossing on a mimic sea of wild, weedy growths? Such images throng the mind on recalling the scene and only faintly hint at its beauty and animation. The long, erect white sepals do much to give the alert, tossing look which the flowers wears. The dim light, too, of its secluded haunts, and its snowy purity and freshness, contribute to the impression it makes. The purple tinge is like a stain of wine which has slightly overflowed the brim of the inflated lip or sac and run part way down its snowy sides.—JOHN BURROUGHS, *Riverby*, 1894

This flower is one of a species whose life is threatened owing to the oft-lamented ruthlessness of "flower-pickers." Near Lenox, Mass., there is one locality where the showy lady's-slipper can be found. Fortunately, one would suppose, this spot is known only to a few; but one of the few who possesses the secret is a country boy who *uproots there plants and sells them by the dozen* in Lenox and Pittsfield. The time is not distant when the flower will no longer be found in the shadowy silences of her native haunts, but only, robbed of half her charm, languishing in stiff rows along the garden-path.—Mrs. WILLIAM STARR DANA, *How to Know the Wild Flowers*, 1893

I have never found the Lady's-slipper as beautiful a flower as do nearly all my friends, as did my father and mother, and I was pleased by Ruskin's sharp comment that such a slipper was fit only for very gouty old toes.—ALICE MORSE EARLE, *Old Time Gardens*, 1901

L A M B K I L L. See under LAUREL

L A R K S P U R was given its name because of the shape of the flowers. The long, pointed nectary was likened to the back spur that characterizes the feet of the lark family, and "lark's heel" and "lark's claw" were other nicknames once in common usage.

In the wild, these flowers are native to China, Siberia, Europe, and North America. We have several deep purple larkspurs on the east coast, but the west is their richest territory, where innumerable varieties are found—a fragile red larkspur; a dazzling assortment of desert larkspurs in the southwest; tiny, low-growing larkspur with fuzzy leaves found northward toward British Columbia; and in the mountains, several species that reach ten feet in height.

The term larkspur is interchangeable with delphinium, the scientific name for this family. But delphinium is usually reserved for the garden varieties. Again, the name was given because of the shape of the blossom. In Greek it was *delphinion,* or "little dolphin," because the long nectary was likened to the nose of the *delphis* or dolphin.

In ancient medicine, larkspur was said to drive away scorpions and other stinging or venomous creatures, and larkspur lotion was once a popular American patent medicine for body lice.

PRAIRIE LARKSPUR

We have two well-marked scarlet species; but confusion still reigns among the blue and white. Some of the latter are poisonous to sheep and cattle, causing great losses to the herds. . . . Among the blue larkspurs are some of our handsomest spring flowers. Their slender wands, covered with magnificent large blossoms, rise abundantly on every side, making charming flower-gardens upon the plains. They are so lavishly bestowed that every comer may gather his fill and still none be missed. In color they are matchless—of the richest Mazarin blue and purple-blue. The Spanish-Californians have a pretty title for these blossoms—"espuela del caballero"—the cavalier's spur.—MARY ELIZABETH PARSONS, *Wild Flowers of California,* 1900

L A U R E L—Most of us are familiar with the myth of the laurel tree, which tells the story of Apollo in pursuit of a reluctant nymph named Daphne. She called for help to her father, the river god, and as Apollo seized Daphne in his arms, the nymph was transformed into a laurel tree.

Our mountain laurels are quite another species, but the name was borrowed because of a similarity between the leaves of the European trees and the American shrubs. Local nicknames were inevitable, such as calico bush which was prompted by the bright markings on the petals, reminiscent of calico prints. Lambkill and sheepkill were given to the dwarf laurel, with deep crimson blossoms, because of the leaves' poisonous properties. One or two drops of a tincture of dwarf laurel was said to be powerful enough to kill a rattler on the spot, and a brew of the leaves was once used as a wash to destroy ticks and fleas on dogs. Wicky is another popular nickname for dwarf laurel, but its origin is unknown.

The botanic name for our laurels is *Kalmia*, given by Linnaeus in honor of Peter Kalm, the Swedish naturalist and a former student of Linnaeus, who visited America in the 1700's. Here is his own report on the plant that bears his name.

Laurel Trees. The spoon tree, which never grows to a great height, was seen to-day. The Swedes here have named it thus, because the Indians used to make their spoons and trowels of its wood. The English call this tree a "laurel" because its leaves resemble those of the *Laurocerasus.* Dr. Linné, because of the friendship and kindness with which he has always honored me has been pleased to call this tree *Kalmia latifolia.* [*Latifolia =* "widespread leaves"] . . . About the month of May they begin to flower, and then their beauty rivals that of most of the known trees in nature. The flowers are innumerable, and grow in great clusters. Before they open they have a fine red color, but as they expand, the sun bleaches them so that some are almost white; many keep the color of roses. Their shape is singular, for they resemble ancient cups. Their scent, however, is none of the most agreeable. In some place it is customary to decorate the churches on Christmas Day or New Year's Day with the fine branches.

But these trees are known for another remarkable quality; their leaves are poison to some animals, and food for others. When sheep eat of these leaves, they either die immediately or fall very sick, and recover with great difficulty. The same noxious effect is observed on calves. . . . Horses, oxen, and cows, have likewise been very ill. . . . On the other hand, the leaves of the *Kalmia* are the food of stags, when the snow covers the ground and hides all other provisions from them. Therefore, if they be shot in winter, their bowels are found filled with these leaves; and it is very extraordinary that if those bowels are then given to dogs, they become stupid, act as if drunk, and often fall so sick that they seem to be at the point of death. But the people who have eaten the venison have not felt the slightest indisposition . . .

The wood of the *Kalmia* is very hard, and some people on that account make the axes of their pulleys of it. Weaver's shuttles are made chiefly of it, and the weavers are of the opinion that no wood in this country is better for the purpose, for it may be made very smooth, and does not easily crack or burst. The joiners and turners here use it in all kinds of work which requires the best wood. . . . The chimney sweepers make brooms in winter of the branches with the leaves on them. In the summer of the year 1750, a certain kind of worm devoured the leaves of almost all the trees in Pennsylvania; yet they did not venture to attack those of the *Kalmia*. Some people assert that when a fire broke out in the woods, it never went beyond the *Kalmias* or spoon trees.—Peter Kalm, *Travels into North America, 1748–1751*

Barewood Gardens, the beautiful home of the editor of the London *Times*, is celebrated for its fine specimens of mountain-laurel . . . The English papers advertise the approach of the flowering season, the estate is thrown open to the public, and people for miles around flock to see the radiant strangers from across the water. The head gardener of the place received with some incredulity my statement that in parts of America the waste hillsides were brilliant with its beauty every June.—Mrs. William Starr Dana, *How to Know the Wild Flowers,* 1893

L I C H E N comes from the Greek verb, *leichein,* to lick or lick up, because these plants "lick" their way across rocks and trees. The name is an ancient one that was officially chosen as a botanic designation in 1700 by Joseph de Tournefort, a French scientist. Something in the neighborhood of 16,000 kinds of lichen grow throughout the world. In the arctic, lichens have served as food for the Eskimo and for starving explorers. In the Orient, certain maritime rock lichens are prized as a delicacy. And Biblical scholars often identify lichens as the manna from heaven which the Israelites found in the wilderness on the flight from Egypt.

A hundred years ago, lichens were still believed to be mosses.

Their true structure was not even guessed at, until researchers gradually discovered that the lichen was two plants in one: a fungus and an alga living in symbiosis, neither able to survive without the other. Long before Beatrix Potter created Peter Rabbit and Flopsy, Mopsy, and Cottontail, she did some original research into the mysteries of lichens—with drawings—but her work was offhandedly dismissed by the high panjandrums of British botany. She put her scientific notebooks aside and later went into the fantasy world of children's stories.

But because lichens were thought to be mosses, many of them carry the wrong name, such as our spongy, gray-green reindeer moss, a staple article of diet for nomadic caribou in the north. *Usnea,* the gray trailing "tree moss," is a lichen, and its name comes from the Arabic *ushna,* or moss. (Spanish moss, by the way, which hangs from our southern trees, is neither a moss *nor* a lichen, but belongs—of all things—to the pineapple family).

Other of our native lichens are "British soldiers," easily identified because the small gray branchlets are topped with red coats. Pyxie cups are similar, but wear no red. Rocktripe, the curling parchment-like lichen, is brown in dry weather and green after a rain. The list is unending: red blanket lichen, whitewash lichen, lollipop lichen, orange star lichen, shell lichen, toad skin lichen, horsehair lichen, ladder lichen . . .

The alga, in the lichen, does the green business, the photosynthesis; the fungus provides water, preventing the other from

PYXIE CUPS

drying out. More, it carries the delicate aquatic alga into realms that are the dryest on earth. Upon my desk lies a stone from Death Valley, not as big as my fist; it is covered with lichens, green gray, red, brown, black—a specialist has identified them as six species. Since I brought home my stone a year ago they have never had water, and they are living still. The lichens go higher in the Himalayas than all other plants; they are almost the only plant life upon the antarctic continent. No jungle growth endures more shade, no desert herb more sun. . . . When the lichen bears fruit or drops off one of its buds, the minute ball of hyphae bears away with it a few green cells of the algae. Together the two partners will roll or blow away, locked in each other's arms in a sort of love and hate, out of which a new lichen will be born, to scale mountain peaks and clothe the lonely forests in sage mourning. There seems to be no condition that these strange plants will not endure, except the fumes of our industrial civilization. —Donald Culross Peattie, *Almanac for Moderns*, 1935, and *Flowering Earth*, 1939

> There is a place of trees . . . gray with lichen.
> I have walked there
> > thinking of old days.
> > > —Ezra Pound, 1885–1972

L I C O R I C E means "sweet root." The Latin word was *liquiritia,* a variation on the original Greek name *glycyrrhiza—* from *glykys,* sweet, and *rhiza,* root. (*Glykys* is also the source word for glycerin.)

Dried roots of the European licorice have been used for countless centuries in cough syrups and laxatives and in confections. When the white man took to producing tobacco, licorice was one of the first flavorful additives. In fact, the plant's flavor is its most valuable asset. Licorice has the remarkable quality of masking the taste of even the most unpalatable medical elixirs.

There is a species of true licorice native to America, growing principally to the westward, from New Mexico to Hudson's Bay. Licorice belongs to the legume family, along with peas and beans, and has white or blueish pea-like blossoms and flat pods. Our other "wild licorice" were given that name because their roots have a similar flavor; country children often pull them to chew on. But they are plants you can easily miss—tiny four-petaled flowers, the leaves in whorls of four, and they belong to the bedstraw family, all of which have weak reclining stems and tend to lie sideways in the grass, while the true licorice grows straight up, two and three feet tall.

Of Liquorice. These plants do grow in sundry places of Germany wilde, and in France and Spaine, but they are planted in gardens in England, whereof I have plenty in my garden: the poore people of the north parts of England do manure it with great diligence, whereby they obtain great plenty thereof.—JOHN GERARD, *Herbal*, 1597

Missouri River Valley. The liquorice of this country does not differ from that common to the United States. It here delights in a deep, loose, sandy soil, and grows very large and abundantly. It is prepared by roasting in the embers, and pounding it slightly with a small stick, in order to separate the strong ligament in the centre of the root, which is then thrown away, and the rest chewed and swallowed. In this way it has an agreeable flavour, not unlike that of the sweet potatoe.—MERIWETHER LEWIS, *The Lewis and Clark Expedition*, 1804–1806

L I L Y. See DAYFLOWER and DAY LILY

L I V E - F O R E V E R. See ORPINE

L I V E R W O R T. See HEPATICA

L O B E L I A—The name was first given to this worldwide family of flowers by Charles Plumier, a French naturalist who botanized in the West Indies in the 1600's. He named the species he found there in honor of Matthias L'Obel, a Flemish physician and botanist to James I. When Linnaeus was reclassifying plants in the next century, he approved of Plumier's choice and kept L'Obel's name as the scientific title.

There used to be a popular misunderstanding about these flowers and their name. Patent medicines in the 1800's, for example, would often specify whether the formula was made up from the smaller varieties, the "low-belias," or the taller varieties, the "high-belias." Actually, the highest of the lobelias, native to the slopes of Mount Kilimanjaro in Tanzania, is a giant wildflower that grows up to twelve feet in height.

Among our native lobelia is the CARDINAL FLOWER. The others are typically a purple-blue, such as Indian tobacco, so-named because of its tobacco scent, and once used to allay asthma. The handsomest is the great lobelia, which you will suddenly come upon blueing a roadside ditch or a marshy meadow. This is the *Lobelia siphilitica*, thus named because the Indians used it as a specific for syphilis.

> They have the venereal disease amongst them in some of its stages. . . . The white traders, themselves say, as well as the Indians, that it might be eradicated if the traders did not carry it with them. . . . These contract the disorder before they set off, and it generally becomes virulent by the time they arrive, when they apply to the Indian doctors to get cured. . . . The Cherokees use the Lobelia siphilitica.—WILLIAM BARTRAM, *Observations on the Creek and Cherokee Indians*, 1789

> *To Stop Hair Falling Out.* Fill a bottle with lobelia roots and stems, and cover well with good whisky, and let stand until digested; then strain off the liquor and add any scent desirable. Rub well into the scalp once a day for a week or two, repeating afterward as may be found necessary.

> Years ago the writer's hair was falling out rapidly; being noticed by a stranger, he advised the above dressing, saying his hair was falling out rapidly, and was not only stopped falling out but had grown in thick by this remedy, and would warrant it to do so in my case. It was immediately used as directed, with the most satisfactory results.—D. MAGNER, *The New System*, 1883

For a score of years I could find the blue spikes of the Great Lobelia in five minutes on any August day by walking from my home to the shady border of Dodge's Pond in Riverdale, but the pond has vanished and the flowers with it. In my life-time I have seen a continued filling-in of bogs and ponds and a covering-over of brooks and streams . . . some of our finest native flowers have disappeared as a result.—JOHN KIERAN, *A Natural History of New York City*, 1959

L O C O W E E D was named by the Spanish. It is native to the far west, and I have not been able to learn what the Indians called it in pre-Spanish days, but they must have had an expressive name for this purple, pink, or white flower that drives livestock loco. Not *all* locoweeds are poisonous, but if animals have grazed on the lethal varieties, it often proves fatal; the dire symptoms are a grinding of the jaws, glassy eyes and defective vision, delirium, and emaciation.

It is strictly a Rocky Mountain plant, extending from British America into Texas, leaving the higher elevations occasionally to adorn the plains below. . . . The flowers of this dry region of our country have little odor, but they are famed for their brilliant colors, by which they give a gay and attractive feature to the otherwise dreary scenery of this inland tract. Among this brilliant assemblage our present species occupies no mean place. . . . It always has the same showy head of flowers, thrown up above the silvery foliage.—THOMAS MEEHAN, *The Native Ferns and Flowers of the United States*, 1880

This is good country for cattle, but not for horses. The loco-weed grows here in great abundance; and which when eaten by a horse kills it very soon after. Mr. Sheetz has seen a horse run for about a hundred yards and then drop dead. He believes it is not the plant, but an insect which is found on the under surface of the leaf that does the injury. Little Robe, the Cheyenne Indian chief, says positively that it is the small green insect that does the mischief. Describing the effect Mr. Sheetz says: "After the animal has eaten the leaves for a little while, the animal seems much exhilarated. It is impossible to handle him. He will not drink water for four or five days. When horses commence to recover, water has to be given to them sparingly. When a horse is locoed, it is easily perceived. Loco is a Spanish word, meaning mad, crack-brained, or foolish, which describes the effects of the weed on horses."—*Las Animas Leader*, 1879, Las Animas, Colorado

L O O S E S T R I F E, according to Pliny, was named for Lysimachus, a crony of Alexander the Great and a general in his army. Lysimachus means loosestrife, from the Greek, *lysis*, loosing, and *mache*, strife—a curious name for a general, whose favorite stamping ground was the battle field and who died happy, sword in hand. But Lysimachus was credited with discovering the powers of the plant; hence the use of his name. As Pliny explained it, if loosestrife were placed on the yoke "when the beasts of burden are quarrelsome, it checks their bad temper." Pliny added that the smell of loosestrife also kept snakes away, that crushed loosestrife cured "the sores caused by footwear," and juice from the stem and flowers would dye the hair flaxen.

There are some two hundred kinds of loosestrife, principally found in eastern Asia and North America. As a general rule, they grow in spires with yellow or pink-purple flowers, and among our native plants are whorled loosestrife, prairie loosestrife, fringed loosestrife, yellow loosestrife or swamp-candle, and wing-angled loosestrife. Among the alien varieties from overseas are MONEYWORT and purple loosestrife, which—to date—has spread inland from the east coast as far as Minnesota.

> It is believed to take away strife, or debate between the beasts, not only those that are yoked together, but even those that are wild also, by making them tame and quiet . . . if it be either put about their yokes or their necks; which how true, I leave to them shall try.—JOHN PARKINSON, 1597–1650, *Paradisi in Sole*

A choice and brilliant purple, like some invasion of metropolitan fashion into a rural congregation, is given to a near-by marsh by the purple loosestrife. During the latter half of August the bog is all aflame with it. There is a wonderful style about this plant, either singly or in masses. . . . The loosestrife is a foreign plant, but it has made itself thoroughly at home here, and its masses of royal purple make the woods look civil and festive.—JOHN BUR-ROUGHS, 1837–1921, *August Days*

L O U S E W O R T. See BETONY

L U P I N E, by its own choice, thrives in poor soil. But in ancient days the concepts of cause and effect were reversed, and it was believed that lupine destroyed the soil, that it wolfed the nourishment out of the earth. Thus it was named after the wolf—*lupus,* in Latin.

The hundreds and hundreds of varieties of lupine belong to the legume family (peas, beans, etc.), and the seeds (like peas and beans, etc.) have been used as food in the Mediterranean countries down over the centuries—the seeds soaked to remove their bitterness and then boiled down into a mush. Wolf's bean was an old name for the plant, and the flat seeds were also used in Roman theater as stage money or by children as counters in games or as play money.

Among the American nicknames for our many varieties—pink, red, white, yellow, blue—are buffalo clover; old maid's bonnet;

LUPINE

blue bonnet, as it is known in Texas where lupine is the state flower; and sun dial, because certain varieties turn their leaves to the side at night or close them around the stalk. The first cultivation of the American lupines was in English nurseries. The *Lupinus ornatus*, for example, with silvery foliage and blue or lilac racemes, was found by David Douglas (See MARIPOSA) in the western mountains and grown by the Horticultural Society of London in 1827. Russell lupines, among the most favored of garden stock, were developed from western American plants by George Russell, a Yorkshire railroad guard, who began his experiments in cross-breeding early in the 1900's and presented the culmination of his years of loving work at an exhibit of the Royal Horticultural Society given in celebration of the coronation of George VI, 1937.

In the lean rocky soil of Maine, where these flowers thrive in the wild, their presence is commemorated by a Coast Guard buoy tender, out of Rockland, that bears the name of *White Lupine*.

June 8, 1852. The Lupine is now in its glory. It is the more important because it occurs in such extensive patches, even an acre or more together. . . . It paints a whole hillside with its blue, making such a field, if not a meadow, as Proserpine might have wandered in. It leaf was made to be covered with dewdrops. . . . Such a profusion of the heavenly, the Elysian color, as if these were the Elysian Fields. That is the value of the Lupine. The earth is blued with it. You may have passed here a fortnight ago and the field is comparatively barren. Now you come here, and these glorious redeemers appear to have flashed out here all at once. Who plants the seeds of Lupines in the barren soil? Who watereth the Lupines in the field? Gray says the name is from lupus, wolf, because they "were thought to devour the fertility of the soil." This is scurrilous.—HENRY DAVID THOREAU, *Journals*

If an Arctic summer is exceptionally cold, some "snow-bed" plants may not emerge at all from underneath deep drifts. But they survive, biding their time for another, more favourable year. . . . Buried in permafrost, they can survive millennia. A lemming's cache of Arctic lupine seeds, hidden deep in the frozen ground more than ten thousand years ago, was recently discovered by botanists. Given earth and light and water, these seeds, asleep for one hundred centuries, awoke to life; they germinated, grew roots and flowers and new seeds. These delicate, lovely plants were older than mankind's recorded history.—FRED BRUEMMER, *Seasons of the Eskimo*, 1971

M A G N O L I A—Although magnolias are usually classified as trees, they are often listed in wildflower books because they were among the first, if not *the* first of our flowering plants. Fossil magnolias, found in such divergent places as Greenland and Java, date from the *Cretaceous* period when the dinosaurs, toothed birds, and flying reptiles died out and covered-seed plants arose—as opposed to the earlier spore-bearing plants, such as the ferns.

Asia and America are still the native habitat of magnolias. One of the first to reach England in the 1600's was swamp bay, the sweet magnolia of our east coast. It was sent to the Bishop of London, an ardent gardener, by John Bannister, a young minister in Virginia who was equally ardent as a botanist and explorer. Another European devoted to the magnolia was Etienne Soulange-Bodin, one of Napoleon's retired officers, whose gardens produced the hybrid *Magnolia soulangeana*. In 1819 he wrote: "To gardens I cheerfully devote the remainder of my life. I shall not retrace the sad picture of the past. The Germans have encamped in my garden. I have encamped in the gardens of the Germans. It had doubtless been better for both parties to have stayed at home and planted their cabbages."

It should be noted that not all the magnolias are beauties. There are any number with flowers that can only be described as interesting in a curious, primeval way.

The name was given by Linnaeus. Magnolia, he wrote, is a

"tree with very handsome leaves and flowers, recalling the splendid botanist Pierre Magnol, professor of Botany and Director of the Montpellier Botanic Garden."

About two leagues from Natchez the road entered an extensive forest, winding along upon a ridge thickly covered with the polished leaved magnolia tree (M. grandiflora)—the pride of southern forests. This tree is an evergreen, and rises from the ground often to the height of seventy feet. . . . The flower is magnificent. When full blown it is of a great size; some of them cannot be placed in a hat without crushing them. Its petals are a pure white. . . . They are frequently used by boarding-school misses to serve as *billets doux*, for which, from their fragrance and unsullied purity, they are admirably fitted. They are so large that I have written upon one of them with a lead pencil in ordinary handwriting, a stanza from Childe Harold. . . . They are so fragrant that a single flower will fill a house with the most agreeable perfume; and the atmosphere for many rods in the vicinity of a tree in full flower is so heavily impregnated, that a sensation of faintness will affect one long remaining within its influence.—Joseph Holt Ingraham, *The South-West, by a Yankee*, 1835

The past week we have been engrossed by magnolias. On Monday our friend D——, armed and equipped with scaling-ladders, ascended the glistening battlements of the great forest-palaces fronting his cottage, and bore thence the white princesses, just bursting into bud, and brought them down to us. . . . We bore them to our chamber, and before morning the whole room was filled with the intoxicating, dreamy fragrance; and while we slept, the pearly hinges had revolved noiselessly, and the bud we had left the evening before had become a great and glorious flower. Imagine a thick, waxen-cupped peony of the largest size, just revealing in its centre a orange-colored cone of the size of a walnut. Around it, like a circlet of emeralds, were the new green leaves, contrasting in their vivid freshness with the solid, dark-green brilliancy of the old foliage. . . . Then we thought of the great lonely swamps and everglades where thousands of these beauties are now bursting into flower with no earthly eye to behold them.—Harriet Beecher Stowe, *Palmetto-Leaves*, 1873

April 25, 1879. What a spring! The white flowers of the magnolias are shivering painfully like women in low dresses sitting in a draught.—EDMOND and JULES DE GONCOURT, *Journal des Goncourt*

M A L L O W comes from the Greek word for these plants —*malache*—which is apparently akin to *malakos,* meaning soft. The name was given either because of the soft downy leaves or because of the soothing, gelatinous properties of the roots, used in cough syrups until quite recently and for "internal irritations," as old medical books put it. Pliny even went so far as to say that one spoonful of syrup, from any of the mallows, would free you from all disease from that day forth. And yes, marshmallows were indeed made from the roots of the marsh mallow once upon a time. But nowadays, according to the packages on the grocer's shelf, they are made of corn syrup, sugar, gelatine, starch, and something called sodium hexametaphosphate.

The lovely white and lavender marsh mallows that grow wild in such pretty profusion on the east coast were originally European. So was the creeping common mallow, the little dooryard plant nicknamed "cheeses," with the small round green cheese-shaped seeds that country children love to eat. Among our native

MARSH MALLOW

species are the big, beautiful rose-mallows, that were sent to England for cultivation in the 1700's.

The French word for mallow is *mauve,* and this eventually became the name of that particular shade of pink, which is the same as the color of the flowers the French had in mind. (The best definition I've heard for mauve is "pink trying to be purple.") *Malache,* the Greek root word for mallow, is also the root for malachite—the ore of copper—because it's the same shade of green as mallow leaves.

> *Kansas.* The Valley of the Little Blue has not presented any great novelty in the way of flowers, but for a splendid variety of the Mallow, of a bright carmine color, its trailing stems sending up flowers in little patches a few yards square, presenting a rich and beautiful appearance and enlivening the monotony of the prairies by its brilliant hues. The root resembles the parsnip and is eaten by the Indians.—CAPT. HOWARD STANSBURY, *Expedition to the Great Salt Lake,* 1849

The only thing I have seen in this country that calls to mind the green grain fields of Britain splashed with scarlet poppies may be witnessed in August in the marshes of the lower Hudson, when the broad sedgy and flaggy spaces are sprinkled with the great marsh mallow. It is a most pleasing spectacle—level stretches of dark green flag or waving marsh grass kindled on every square yard by the bright pink blossoms, like great burning coals fanned in the breeze. The mallow is not so deeply colored as the poppy, but it is much larger and has the tint of youth and happiness. It is an immigrant from Europe, but it is making itself at home in our great river meadows.—JOHN BURROUGHS, *Riverby,* 1894

Our path led to the kitchen door at the house-end, and there grew a mass of gay flowers and greenery, as if they had been swept together by some diligent garden broom. There were portulaces all along under the lower step, and clustering mallows that crept as near as they dared like poor relations. I saw the bright eyes and brainless little heads of two half-grown chicks who were snuggled down among the mallows, as though they had been chased away from the door more than once, and expected to be again.—SARAH ORNE JEWETT, *The Country of the Pointed Firs*, 1896

Rose Mallow, a marvel of beauty in coastal marshes from Florida to Massachusetts and westward as far as Lake Erie. I have known this lusty six-footer intimately since boyhood, yet I can convey no more than a suggestion of its loveliness when it comes into bloom in the latter days of summer. Imagine, if you will, a vast sea of green marsh grass and Cat-tails rippling in a fresh August breeze. Floating a little above it is a second sea of pink—the untold millions of the Mallows. And infinitely far above all this the deep blue arch of the sky and a white fleet of slowly drifting clouds.—ROBERT S. LEMMON, *Wildflowers of North America*, 1961

M A R I G O L D—Like lady's-slipper, this was a name given in dedication to the Virgin. The original meaning was "Mary's Gold," and over the centuries it has been a favorite nickname for any number of yellow flowers. It's a pretty, all-purpose word. In early England, marigold was an alternate name for calendula, the ancient pot-herb that pepped up stews, gravies, puddings, etc. (Calendula comes from a Latin word meaning the first days of every month—the *calends*—because the plant was said to bloom only at those times.) The English also gave the marigold name to their golden, early-spring, marsh flowers, and it was handed on to the American marsh marigolds, or COWSLIP.

In the southwest, there is the bright yellow-orange daisy-like "desert marigold" that will bloom the year round; we also have bur-marigolds, corn marigolds, fetid marigolds, and rayless marigolds or beggar-ticks—this last nickname, because the barbed seedpods catch on cloth or animal fur and thereby "beg" their way to new breeding grounds.

However, none of these wild flowers are the true marigold, as far as botanists are concerned. True marigolds belong to the *Tagetes* family, named for Tages, a grandson of Jupiter who taught the Etruscans the meaning of lightning, winds, eclipses, and other natural phenomena. *Tagetes* are native to Mexico and South America and were discovered by the Spanish, who brought them home from the New World. From Spain, they were taken to Africa—perhaps for a Moorish garden—and there they spread in the hospitable African climate and grew wild along the northern shores.

When this attractive new flower became known to the English, they gave it their all-purpose name, marigold, because it was similar to pot-marigold, the calendula of ancient days. To add to the historic confusion of when and where, this transplanted Spanish-American wildflower was specifically known in England as the "African marigold" and another smaller variety, that made its way north by way of France, was called the "French marigold." They became favorite garden flowers, extensively hybridized, and to this day are generally known as French or African marigolds.

Meanwhile, in Mexico they still grow wild and are known as the *flor de muerto,* the flower of death, and are gathered to decorate graves on the Day of the Dead. According to Mexican folklore, marigolds sprang from the blood of the Indians slaughtered by Cortes, and each flower that bloomed was there to remind the next generation to avenge their forefathers' ignoble deaths.

But there is one more chapter to the marigold saga. The late Everett McKinley Dirksen, senator from Illinois, tried for years to have the marigold named our national flower. In his undaunted crusade, the senator specified the *Tagetes erecta,* which is the *flor de muerto* in Mexico and the African marigold in seed catalogues. It was an odd choice for the senator to have set his heart on.

From the Congressional Record, February 4, 1969, here is a transcript—notable for its wealth of patriotic misinformation.

Mr. DIRKSEN . . . For some years I have been carrying the flag in cause, and that cause is to have the American marigold—*Tagetes erecta*—officially designated by the Congress as the national floral emblem of the United States. . . . I am fully sensible of the fact that all persons, young and old, male and female, rich and poor, have their own preferences when it comes to a flower. But mine goes for the marigold for a variety of reasons. It is actually an

American native and really not native to any other place on earth. It is grown in great profusion in every one of the 50 States. . . . Long ago it was acknowledged as a symbol of religious faith and graced the altars both at home and abroad.

One of the outstanding characteristics of the marigold is its robustness and rugged character. If there is any flower that can resist the onslaught of the insect world better than the marigold, I would not know what it was. I grow thousands of them every year for my own delight and the delight of my neighbors, and I know what this flower will do.

I class it, therefore, with the American eagle when it comes to a symbol of our country that manifests stamina; and when it comes to beauty, I can think of nothing greater or more inspiring than a field of blooming marigolds tossing their heads in the sunshine and giving a glow to the entire landscape. . . . Like the American eagle and the American flag, [the marigold is] an exclusively American emblem, unclaimed by any foreign nation. . .

M A R I P O S A—A unique genus of some fifty incredibly beautiful flowers, native to the western half of our continent. The name means butterfly in Spanish, because the markings on the petals of certain mariposas are like the markings on butterfly wings, and butterfly tulip is one of their nicknames. The sego lily, Utah's state flower, is a mariposa, and its edible roots, long eaten by the Indians, were one of the survival foods found in the wilderness by Mormon settlers. Sego is a Shoshonean word of no known meaning.

Mariposas, in all their variations, go from white, lilac, pink, and claret, to purple, red-orange, and yellow. Some are solid colors, others are specked with contrasting colors—green, cream, lilac, or red. Some have open blooms like the tulip. Others are star-shaped. Still others have fringed petals. Some have round nodding heads and are known as globe tulips, globe lilies, or fairy lanterns.

Lewis and Clark brought back dried specimens of the mariposa. But the first living collection was made by David Douglas, a young Scotsman who traveled in search of new plants for the

MARIPOSA LILY

Royal Horticultural Society in London. During his various trips through the Hudson's Bay territory, Alaska, British Columbia, and western America, from 1823 to 1833, Douglas gathered three hundred and forty new species of American flora and was known to the Indians as the Big Grass Man. The Douglas fir is his tree. In fact, he discovered so many American trees that he wrote to a friend, "You will think I manufacture Pines at my pleasure." In 1834, when botanizing in the Philippines, Douglas fell into a pit dug to catch wild cattle. A bull, already caught in the trap, gored him to death. One of the last flowers he had sent to England, before sailing to the Philippines, was a yellow mariposa collected in California, and it was duly planted in the Royal Horticultural Garden at Chiswick. This is the variety of mariposa described in a quote from an English periodical.

> We have so long considered the Mariposa Lilies somewhat delicate and fragile . . . we are agreeably surprised at finding they keep for considerable time in water, and open their large, gay, yet delicately marked blooms freely. The ones before us are of a fine dazzling yellow color, with brownish-crimson pencillings and markings.—*London Garden*, July 1, 1876

The mountain's side faced south and had no shade, and the sun was at its hotest . . . a purple mystery of mountains and canon dreaming in the wistful haze of summer; at five miles' distance the inifinite plain of the sea shone softly under the southern sun. . . . On nearing the summit, oaks began to appear, often surrounded with lakelets of tender grass. Here I found growing freely the lovely globe tulip, a white saint of a flower, all ethereal gentleness and tranquillity, the purest looking blossom I know. I think a pirate would look at it with reverence.—J. SMEATON CHASE, *California Coast Trails*, 1913

Very few have succeeded in growing the Mariposa Tulips with ordinary culture, either in America or Holland, as we remarked in a recent number, but E. Hutzelen of Le Roy, N.Y., seems to be more lucky, for he writes: "I have a fine bed of Mariposa containing all the varieties shown in *Album von Eeden*. The soil in which they grow is a coarse quicksand enriched with a very little swamp muck. They are planted six inches deep. I never disturb them nor cover them in winter, and they come thicker every year, most of them growing two feet high and going to seed. They are less trouble than Tulips. Plenty of sand with a dry bottom, and full sunshine for three parts of the day seem to be all they need. I have also found that manure from the barnyard will do them more harm than good. With the exception of pulling the weeds, the treatment by which I succeed is to *let them alone.*" —E. HUZTELEN, *Vick's Magazine*, September, 1878

MARSH ROSEMARY—A misty lavender, late-blooming flavor that grows along the American coastline from Newfoundland to Texas; sea lavender is another popular name. In early days, it was known as inkroot, because the roots yield tannic acid, used in ink, dyes, and the tanning of leather. Canker root, or cankerwort, was another early nickname, in reference to its medical value in the cure of canker sores and similar afflictions. Marsh rosemary has always been used for winter bouquets; the flowers keep their delicate color when dried and also were reputed to be a moth repellent. Beauty and practicality in one.

This sea-side plant is not to be confused with the true rosemary,

Rosemary officinalis, an ancient Mediterranean herb. The name was borrowed, and fittingly, too, since the Mediterranean rosemary was believed to have sprung from the sea spray, as did Venus. Ovid called it *Rosmaris,* Pliny called it *Rosmarinum,* and early English writers called it *Rosmarine*—all from the Latin *ros,* dew, and *marinus,* marine. In other words, it was "sea-dew." With the Christian era, the plant became associated with the Virgin, because of the sound of the word *rosmarine.* It was Mary's rose, or rosemary, and a new legend grew up—much like the legend of Mahomet and the GERANIUM. It was said that the Virgin washed her blue cloak one day and laid it to dry over a rosemary bush. For ever after the flowers were as blue as her cloak.

Besides being a borrowed name for our marsh rosemary, it's also used for an ANDROMEDA that's often called bog-rosemary.

> Inland from the sea there are unceasing changes of color throughout the year. The black grass is the first to flower; its fruit turns brown quite early in the summer. The salt-marsh reeds and grasses are blue-green and yellow-green in the summer, red and tawny and gold in the fall. . . . At the same time, the sea lavender or marsh rosemary is blooming—a bouquet in itself with light woody stems and a profusion of small, delicate, lavender-blue flowers. . . .
> —JOHN HAY and PETER FARB, *The Atlantic Shore,* 1966

> "This was what she called the best room; in this way," he said presently. . . . The best room seemed to me a much sadder and more empty place than the kitchen. It was only when one remembers what patient saving goes into such furnishings that the little parlor was interesting at all. I could imagine the great day of certain purchases, the bewildering shops of the next large town, the aspiring anxious woman, the clumsy sea-tanned man in his best clothes, at ease only when they were safe back in the sail-boat again, going down the bay with their precious freight, the hoarded money all spent. . . . I looked at the unworn carpet, the glass vases on the mantelpiece with their prim bouquets of bleached swamp grass and dusty marsh rosemary, and I could read the history of Mrs. Tilley's best room from its very beginning.—SARA ORNE JEWETT, *The Country of the Pointed Firs,* 1897

M A Y P O P. See Passion Flower

M I L K W E E D was given its name because the stems of most of our American varieties exude a sticky milky-white juice. This seems to be nature's device to keep crawling insects away from the flowers, since milkweed depends upon flying insects for pollenization. When an ant, for example, crawls up a milkweed stalk, it makes minute holes enroute and in no time is bogged down with gummy mittens of milkweed sap, which begins to harden like glue as soon as the air hits it. Ants have been observed trying to clean off their feet, the struggle only producing more minute holes in the stalk and more of the milky juice—a losing battle for any invader.

Milkweeds also have a unique arrangement for pollenization. Their tiny pollen sacks are linked together like saddlebags, and when a bee or butterfly lands on the flower head and stumbles for its footing on the slippery petals, the pollen "saddle-bags" are hooked over their legs. At the next flower, the pollen sacks break away and are left behind, and the process is repeated, the bee or

COMMON MILKWEED

butterfly departing with a new cargo of pollen sacks dangling from its ankles to take to the next flower. And so on, from flower to flower.

We have varieties of milkweed with white blossoms, deep purple-red, and orange, such as the BUTTERFLY WEED, but the most familiar throughout America is our common milkweed with powdery, lavender-colored flower heads.

> *Common Milkweed.* The French in Canada use its tender shoots in spring, preparing them like asparagus. . . . Its flowers are very fragrant, and, when in season, they fill the woods with their sweet exhalations and make it agreeable to travel in them, especially in the evening. The French in Canada make a sugar of the flowers, which for that purpose are gathered in the morning, when they are covered with dew. This dew is pressed out, and by boiling yields a very good brown, palatable sugar. The pods of this plant when ripe contain a kind of wool, which encloses the seed and resembles cotton. . . . The poor collect it and with it fill their beds, especially their children's, instead of feathers. This plant flowers at the end of June and the beginning of July, and the seeds are ripe in the middle of September. The horses never eat this plant.—PETER KALM, *Travels into North America,* 1748–1751

MILKWORT. See under POLYGALA and WORT

MINT—The name comes from Mentha, a naiad who was the mistress of Pluto, ruler of Hades; she was trampled underfoot by Pluto's jealous queen, Proserpine, and transformed into a lowly plant that would be walked upon forever after. Mentha's fate, however, was softened by Pluto, who willed that the more mint plants were trodden upon, the sweeter the smell that would arise.

The mints are an enormous family, all aromatic, all with square stems, opposite leaves, and irregular two-lipped flowers that are often described as dragon heads. To touch on a few, the water mint, horse mint, catnip, heal-all, GILL-OVER-THE-GROUND, peppermint, spearmint, and bugle (origin unknown), that grow wild in our low meadows or along our streams, are European imports—the Europeans in their turn having imported many mints, particularly peppermint and spearmint, from Asian and Near Eastern gardens. The early Persians and Arabs were the first to use mint as flavoring for their drinks, and that's where "julep" comes from. It was a Persian word meaning rose-water—*gulab*, from *gul*, or rose, and *ab*, or water. Eventually, it came to mean a drink sweetened with any sort of aromatic herb, but particularly with mint.

Pliny wrote, "The smell of mint doth stir up in the mind and taste a greedy desire for meat." Horsemint was chewed by the Romans as an active remedy against the parasitic worm that caused elephantiasis. Dioscorides in *De Materia Medica* spoke of mint "as an enemy to generation by overthickening seed . . . and being applied to the secret part of a woman before the act, it hindreth conception." In early English herbals, mints were recommended as "friendly to the weak Stomach and powerful against all nervous crudities." Further, "Mints were ever a good posie for students to smell of, for it quickens the brain." And, "The savour or smell of the Water-Mint rejoiceth the heart of man. . ."

Meantime in America, from unrecorded ages past, the Indians also used the native mints in similar ways—in teas to allay fevers and to settle the stomach, and in soothing liniments. The scent of mint that rejoiced medieval hearts rejoiced Indian hearts as well; they used native mints such as BERGAMOT to scent bear grease hair-dressings. Our native DITTANY and PENNYROYAL were useful as bug repellants, and at one time American farmers packed mint with their stored grain to keep away rats and mice. As for the imported spearmint, it became an important commercial crop, particularly after chewing gum took over the American scene; as early as 1890, many Europeans believed that every American chewed spearmint gum through every waking hour.

The American mint julep, however, delighted overseas visitors. When Charles Dickens toured the United States in 1842, he wrote, with great wistfulness: "The bowls of mint juleps they make in these latitudes are refreshments never to be thought of afterwards, in summer, by those who would preserve contented minds." Mrs. Trollope, also an English visitor, felt the same.

It would, I truly believe, be utterly impossible for the art of man to administer anything so likely to restore them from the overwhelming effects of heat and fatigue, as a large glass filled to the brim with the fragrant leaves of nerve-restoring mint, as many solid lumps of delicately pellucid, crystal-looking ice, as it can conveniently contain, a proper proportion of fine white sugar, (not beetroot), and then—I would whisper it gently, if I knew how—a whole wine-glass full of whiskey poured upon it, to find its insinuating way among the crystal rocks, and the verdant leaves, till by gentle degrees, a beverage is produced that must create a delicious sensation of coolness, under a tropical sun, and a revival of strength, where strength seemed gone for ever.—MRS. FRANCES TROLLOPE, *The Old World and the New*, 1849

The poets tell us that Proserpine, Pluto's wife, in a fit of jealousy changed a hated rival into the mint plant. . . . How she must delight in seeing her under the chopping-knife and served up as sauce!—NELTJE BLANCHAN, *Nature's Garden*, 1901

In the north pasture, the title "pasture" by courtesy only now, a pool of mint rises each spring, a lavender pond filled with bees, great bumblebees, small yellow bees, and the brown furry bees like winged mice. It is filled with the humming of the bees and the spicy smell of the mint leaves (leaves rich, green, convoluted as seashells) and the pool widens into a wider pool of white pansy violets, like a foam at the far edges. . . . This is the view from the woodchuck's den above the draw.—JOSEPHINE W. JOHNSON, *The Inland Island*, 1969

M I S T L E T O E was originally *misteltan* in Anglo-Saxon and means "the little dung twig." *Mistel* is a diminutive of the German *mist*, or dung, and *tan* is Anglo-Saxon for twig. The name was given because of the part birds play in propogating this parasitic plant, eating the berries in one place and excreting them in another. In fact, it was believed that mistletoe would not sprout at all, unless ripened in the stomachs of birds.

Sacred to the druids of northern Europe, the Ainos of Japan, and certain tribes in Africa, mistletoe was surrounded with mystery and superstition. It was a plant that grew without roots in the ground, as though it had fallen from the sky as a divine gift, and as a divine gift it was likened to the soul, because the mistletoe was evergreen. In Northern winters when the trees "died," the fresh foliage of the mistletoe was the sign of life everlasting; the souls of the trees still lived.

Mistletoe was the all-healer; it protected against witchcraft and nightmares; it evoked ghosts and caused them to answer your questions; it opened all locks, guarded your dairy and stable from trolls, cured epilepsy, warded off death in battle, induced omens of good or bad fortune; and as a divining rod, it pointed the way to buried gold or treasure.

American mistletoe is the state flower of Oklahoma. When the territory was opened to homesteaders in 1889, mistletoe—thick as Spanish moss—filled the forests of the Ozark, Arbuckle, Jack Fork, Kiamichi, and Winding Stair mountains. In winter months it was often the only green plant the pioneers could find to put on the graves of their dead. In 1893, a Mrs. Beason, one of the early settlers in Old Reno City, proposed mistletoe as the Territory flower. There was some stiff opposition in the legislature from church groups; this plant, after all, was a pagan flower by myth and reputation. But the bill passed, though one legislator who voted for mistletoe said, "I do so under protest, as I do not think our valuable time should be taken up in such frivolous business." The day was carried, however, by another legislator's formal approval. "The first winter after the Opening," he told his colleagues, "the woods along the creeks and in the river bottoms were covered with mistletoe, and it was in full bloom at Christmas. It was a delightful vision to those of us who had been raised in the North, and many of the early settlers gathered whole clusters of the beautiful plant and sent it to their friends. We accepted with delight the name bestowed upon our new country—The Land of the Mistletoe."

One of the few things the herbwoman never collects is mistletoe. These clumps usually grow too high in trees. However, much of the mistletoe that reaches northern states during the holiday season comes from North Carolina, tons being shipped from one county alone. Some modern Daniel Boones, expert with a squirrel rifle, are said to harvest the topmost bunches in their own peculiar way, snipping off the branches with well-directed lead.—EDWIN WAY TEALE, *North with the Spring*, 1956

MITREWORT. See under WORT

MOCCASIN FLOWER. See LADY'S-SLIPPER

MONEYWORT, which was introduced from England, now grows wild—with or without encouragement—throughout northeastern and north-central America. The name was given because of its small coin-shaped leaves, and herb tuppence is another nickname in its homeland. Creeping charlie and creeping LOOSESTRIFE are also commonly heard both in England and America.

This free-flowering plant, from its trailing habit, is well fitted for

MONEYWORT

decorating rock-work. It grows in wet meadows, boggy pastures, and the borders of rivulets . . . and affords a wholesome food for cattle, especially sheep. The leaves and flowers of this plant, steeped in oil, furnish an excellent remedy for destroying the worms and insects infesting the floors of granaries.—CUTHBERT W. JOHNSON, ESQ., *The Farmer's and Planter's Encyclopedia*, 1852

Moneywort, a native of Great Britain . . . long a favorite vine in American hanging baskets and urns, suspended from a veranda . . . Pairs of yellow, dark-spotted, five-lobed flowers grow from the axils of the opposite leaves from June to August. One often finds it running wild in moist soil beyond the pale of old gardens. . . . Slight encouragement in starting runaways would easily induce the hardy little evergreen to be as common here as it is in England. —NELTJE BLANCHAN, *Nature's Garden*, 1901

M U G W O R T. See under ARTEMISIA

M U L L E I N is a derivation of the Latin *mollis*, meaning soft, because of the plant's thick gray-green woollen leaves. (*Mollis* also is the root for mollify, emollient, and mollusk—these invertebrate marine creatures were the "soft ones," the *mollusca*.)

There are many varieties of mullein, and all of them are originally native to the Mediterranean region, though not all have the mullein-esque woollen leaves. Some have been cultivated into enormously handsome garden plants, but the most familar of this family is the "common mullein" that grows wild throughout America—a tall ramrod of a plant with scattered yellow flowers that came to us via England and is happy to grow where nothing else will take root. The moth mullein, a smaller variety and another emigré gone native, was given its name because it is particularly attractive to moths and butterflies.

Pliny recommended the common mullein for coughs and tonsilitis. The Romans coated dried mullein stalks with suet and burned them as funeral torches. And when common mullein came to England, it picked up some forty nicknames as it spread its way across the countryside. Here are a few: candlewick, hedge taper, high taper, torches, Aaron's rod, blanket leaf, velvet plant, flannel leaf, Adam's-flannel, old-man's-flannel, hare's-beard, lungwort, and longwort.

The humming bird always builds its nest in the middle of a branch, and it is so small that it cannot be seen from the ground. . . The one in my possession is quite round, and consists on the inside of a brownish and quite soft down, which seems to have been collected from the leaves of the great mullein, which are often found covered with a soft wool of this color, and the plant is plentiful here. . . . The Swedes here tie the leaves round their feet and arms, when they have the ague. Some of them prepared a tea from the leaves for dysentery. A Swede likewise told me that a decoction of the roots was injected into the wounds of cattle when afflicted with worms.—Peter Kalm, *Travels into North America*, 1748–1751

July 8, 1851 . . . Here are mulleins covering a field where three years ago none were noticeable, but a smooth, uninterrupted pasture sod. Two years ago it was ploughed for the first time for many years, and millet and corn and potatoes planted. Now, where the millet grew, these mulleins have sprung up. Who can write the history of these fields? The millet does not perpetuate itself, but the few seeds of the mullein which perchance were brought here with it are still multiplying the race.—Henry David Thoreau, *Journals*

We are afraid of that word "weed," and the name Mullein in the minds of many of us is synonymous with this outlaw term. . . . We do not countenance weeds. But can anyone with an eye for line and color view without interest a raw roadside cut rescued from blatant hideousness by the amazing dignity and beauty of crowding, towering stalks of what we are pleased to call our native Mullein? . . . Garden plants are required to hit you in the eye, so to speak, before they are admissible, and the common Mullein has a stingy way of opening its blossoms one by one, or a few at a time; and so this plant is not deemed fit for garden circles.—Louise Beebe Wilder, *What Happens in My Garden*, 1935

The really delicate and beautiful flowers of this genus are those that the Moth Mullein scatters along its stem. . . . The yellow flowers are held out from the stem on little stalks. . . . What is truly piquant about them is that the upstanding five stamens are bearded with violet hairs in such a way as to give the flowers the appearance of golden butterflies much like the design that the short-tempered and long-feuding James Abbott McNeill Whistler used as a signature—the famous "butterfly remarque"—on many of his paintings, etchings, and lithographs.—JOHN KIERAN, A Natural History of New York City, 1959

M U S H R O O M comes from the French mousseron, which means, in effect, that these plants grow in mousse, or moss —that is to say, in moist places. The word came into English as muscheron, and finally settled down as mushroom. Incidentally, a chocolate mousse gets its name from the Latin mulsus, to be sweet, or, to be mixed with honey.

No one seems to have added up exactly how many thousands upon thousands of varieties of mushrooms grow on this earth, but everyone agrees—and has always agreed—that you shouldn't eat wild mushrooms unless you're an A-1, crackerjack authority on the poisonous species. Pliny described mushrooms as a two-edged sword, and Horace warned, in verse, "The meadow mushrooms are in kind the best/ It is ill trusting any of the rest." The kind we buy in markets today are cultivated "meadow" mushrooms, so Horace's admonition still holds true almost two thousand years later.

The flavor is the thing with mushrooms. They contain some pro-tein and minerals, but are principally made up of water and have very little nutritive value. But their delicate and unique flavor has always been appreciated by connoisseurs. In Roman days, the mushroom was considered a delicacy only for the elite—despite the fact that entire dinner parties of the elite were often carried to their graves in the morning because there had been a slip-up in the kitchen the night before.

Mushrooms belong to the fungus family, and fungus comes from the Greek spongos, or sponge, given as a descriptive name.

FIELD MUSHROOM

For all their striking appearance, the familiar mushrooms are merely the reproductive structures of certain soil-dwelling fungi. The mycelium grows hidden in the soil, foraging on decaying leaves, rotting wood, manure, and other organic matter. After the mycelium has grown sufficiently, and after it has gotten the necessary amount of rain, it forms small buttons which increase in size and appear above the soil surface, where they develop into the characteristic mushrooms. Each has a stalk that supports a cap with gills on its undersurface. These gills produce enormous numbers of spores, as many as two billion per mushroom. . . . When ripe, the spores are popped off the gill. . . . In still air they settle to the ground; when a breeze is stirring they are blown away.—HENRY and REBECCA NORTHEN, *Ingenious Kingdom*, 1970

August, too, is the month of the mushrooms—those curious, abnormal flowers of a hidden or subterranean vegetation, invoked by heat and moisture from darkness and decay as the summer wanes. Do they not suggest something sickly and uncanny in Nature? Her unwholesome dreams and night fancies, her pale superstitions; her myths and legends and occult lore taking shape in them, spectral and fantastic, at times hinting something libidinous and unseemly: vegetables with gills, fibreless, bloodless; earth-flesh, often offensive, unclean, immodest, often of rare beauty and delicacy, of many shades and colors—creamy white, red, yellow, brown—now the hue of an orange, now of a tomato, now of a potato, some edible, some poisonous, some shaped like spread umbrellas, some umbrellas reversed by the wind—the sickly whims and fancies of Nature, some imp of the earth mocking and travestying the things of the day. . . . The decay of a mushroom parodies that of real flesh—a kind of unholy rotting ending in blackness and stench. Some species imitate jelly—mock calves'-foot jelly, which soon melts down and becomes an uncanny mass. Occasionally I see a blue-gilled mushroom—an infusion of indigo in its cells. How forbidding it looks! Yesterday in the August woods, I saw a tiny mushroom like a fairy parasol of a Japanese type—its tops delicately fluted.

During the steaming, dripping, murky, and muggy days of August, how this fungus growth runs riot in the woods and in the fields too—a kind of sacrilegious vegetation mocking Nature's saner and more wholesome handiwork—the flowers of death, vegetable spectres, JOHN BURROUGHS, 1837–1921, *August Days*

M U S T A R D—All plants of the mustard family (the dozens upon dozens of them) have four-petaled flowers in the shape of a rounded Maltese cross, which gives them their Latin name, the *cruciferae*. The four petals are a good key to recognition —a necessary key, in fact, since the mustard family is so vast and its members come in so many shapes, sizes, and colors: DAME'S ROCKET; the small pink or white toothwort (toothed leaves); broccoli ("little sprout," from the Italian, *brocco*); radishes (from the Latin *radix*, or root); watercress; shepherd's purse (from the shape of the seed pods) . . . This family tree could go on and on.

America has its native mustards, but a preponderance of the wild varieties are alien plants of Near Eastern or European origin —such as hedge mustard, Indian mustard, hare's-ear mustard (from the shape of the leaves), field mustard, charlock (origin unknown), black mustard (because of its dark brown seeds), and white mustard (because of its light brown seeds). Both the black and the white mustards, which grow anyplace and everyplace from coast to coast, are the same plants as the commercial crops used in bottled mustards. And here is where the meaning of "mustard" comes in.

The volatile oil that gives the mustard seed its snap is tasteless until mixed with water, wine, vinegar, or whatever. It needs the agency of a liquid to release the flavor. The Greeks, Romans, Egyptians, et al., were aware of this unusual property and they added *must,* or unfermented wine, to the chopped seeds to make a condiment. (*Must,* originally a Latin word, is still used today in English for unfermented grape juice.) In northern Europe, this spicy condiment made of must and chopped seeds became known as must-ard—the *ard* being a Germanic suffix meaning "hard." In other words, this was a hard mixture, as opposed to being a liquid mixture of unfermented wines. Eventually, mustard became the name of the plants that produced the spicy seeds.

The young leaves and the flower buds of black mustard and field mustard are as edible as those of their garden relative, broccoli. Use in a salad, or boil like spinach.

> *Mustard.*—Before the year 1729, powdered mustard was not known at English table. About that time an old woman of the name of Clements, residing in Durham, began to grind the seed in a mill and to pass the flour through several processes necessary to free the seed from its husks. She kept her secret for many years to herself, during which she sold large quantities of mustard throughout the country, but especially in London. Here it was introduced to the royal table, when it received the approval of George I. From the circumstance of Mrs. Clements being a resident at Durham, it obtained the name of Durham mustard. It is the best stimulant employed to impart strength to the digestive organs, and even in its previously coarsely-pounded state, had a high reputation with our ancestors.—Mrs. ISABELLA BEETON, *The Book of Household Management,* 1861

> It is no exaggeration to say that the Common Black Mustard will grow anywhere. I have found it coming up through the cracks in a "hot-topped" parking lot in midtown Manhattan. It is not only persistent and widespread but almost incredibly hardy and I regularly find it in bloom as late as November. For that reason, though its little yellow flowers are nothing to boast of, I long ago put in on my Roll of Honor . . . —JOHN KIERAN, *A Natural History of New York City,* 1959

The wild mustard in Southern California is like that spoken of in the New Testament, in the branches of which the birds of the air may rest. Coming up out of the earth, so slender a stem that dozens can find starting-point in an inch, it darts up a slender, straight shoot, five, ten, twenty feet, with hundreds of fine, feathery branches locking and interlocking with all the other hundreds around it, till it is an inextricable network, like lace. Then it bursts into yellow bloom, still finer, more feathery and lace-like. The stems are so infinitesimally small and of so dark a green, that at a short distance they do not show, and the cloud of blossoms seems floating in the air; at times it looks like a golden dust. With a clear, blue sky behind it, as it is often seen, it looks like a golden snowstorm.
—HELEN HUNT JACKSON, *Ramona,* 1884

M Y R T L E. See PERIWINKLE

N E T T L E—One of Hans Christian Andersen's fairy tales tells the story of eleven princes who were transformed into wild swans. They could be saved only if their sister, the princess, wove them shirts out of stinging nettles. She worked for a year with bleeding fingers, and when the swans returned from the north all the shirts were finished, except for the last, which had only one sleeve. But the time was up. The swans would fly on. The princess threw the nettle shirts over their backs, and her brothers were restored—except for the youngest, whose shirt had only one sleeve. Forever after, the youngest brother had one white wing.

Though this was only a fairy story, nettles have indeed been woven into cloth and twine since time immemorial, and one of the uses of nettle twine was the weaving of nets. Hence, the name nettle or "net plant." The word net has its own interesting origin, beginning with *nezzi* in Old German, which was apparently borrowed from *nassa,* the Latin for fish net, and *nassa* is akin to the Sanskrit *nahyati,* "he binds."

Nettles have also served as food since time immemorial, the young shoots boiled like spinach, and they're still recommended in cookbooks on wild vegetables. Samuel Pepys, in 1661, noted in his diary that a nettle porridge was served to guests, and it was very tasty.

We have a number of native nettles, but the worst offender is an alien from the Old World—the horse-nettle or stinging-nettle. Others—such as the hoary nettle, slender nettle, California nettle, hedge nettle, hemp nettle, and so forth—are less virulent in their bite. The sting is caused by formic acid. Each nettle hair is a tubular cell with a razor-sharp point that breaks off under the skin, and the acid is released, smarting and itching.

> The seed being drank is a remedy against the stinging of venomous creatures, the biting of mad dogs, the poisonous qualities of hemlock, henbane, nightshade, mandrake, or other such herbs that stupify or dull the senses. . . . Nettles are so well known that they need no description; they may be found by feeling in the darkest night.—Dr. Nicholas Culpeper, *English Physician and Complete Herbal,* 1649

> The caustic and detergent properties of the white nettle of Carolina and Florida for cleansing old ulcers and consuming proud flesh were discovered by the Indians to the inhabitants of Carolina. (The white nettle roots are good and wholesome food when roasted and boiled; they are about the size of a large carrot when well grown, but few of them are allowed to become large, the swine are so fond of them.)

> I was informed by the people that, in order to prepare and administer these remedies, they dig up the roots and divide and cut them into three pieces, in order for their more speedy drying in the shade, and then reduce them to powder, [which is] plentifully spread over the ulcer . . . —William Bartram, *Observations on the Creek and Cherokee Indians,* 1789

> In Scotland, I have eaten nettles, I have slept in nettle-sheets, and I have dined off a nettle-tablecloth. The young and tender

nettle is an excellent potherb. The stalks of the old nettle are as good as flax for making cloth. I have heard my mother say, that she thought nettle-cloth more durable than any other species of linen.
—JOSEPH CAMPBELL, 1881–1944

NIGHT-BLOOMING CEREUS—*Cereus* is a family name for certain varieties of cactus native to the western United States and tropical America, and there are several of them famed as night-blooming flowers with a fragrance that has been described as tuberoses, regal lilies, jasmine, and all the sweetest odors in the world mixed together into one perfume. The life of a single flower lasts only a few hours. They bloom in the dark, are pollenized by moths, and fade before dawn.

The name comes from the Latin *cera,* or wax candle, because so many members of this family have columnar shapes like candles. Cactus, from the Greek *kaktos,* has no known meaning.

In Mexican folklore, it is said that the night-blooming cereus time their flowering to honor San Juan's day—June 24, the supposed birthdate of John the Baptist. And the Indians of the southwest call the night-blooming cereus "desert queens."

Every morning and evening when the shade lay in the canyon I made the rounds among my night-blooming plants, a number of which I discovered myself. The buds developed slowly or perhaps I was impatient. But at last came the evening when one was lifting its heavy head. . . . By midnight the moon was sailing high, the canyon almost as bright as day, and we didn't need the lantern, as the three of us followed the gleaming white pathway of the sand-wash. . . .

The bud had swollen considerably and was almost erect on its stem. It was loosening up, the white petals plainly visible in the moonlight. We spread our blankets on the sand and settled down to watch. . . . The bud was expanding in spasmodic jerks and beginning to send off the sweet elusive perfume. We could almost see those creamy petals unfold. The perfume became heady, intoxicating. Breathlessly we watched. The night was still. It seemed to be watching too. At last a full-blown blossom, fully six inches across, gleamed in the white moonlight, its immaculate center filled with hundred of waxy white stamens, yellow tipped, like so many lighted altar candles.

The Queen of the Night was in bloom!

Silently we worshipped. A moth fluttered up, quivered about the glistening petals, and melted away in a moonbeam . . . —OLGA WRIGHT SMITH, *Gold on the Desert*, 1956

ORCHID, or ORCHIS—The name was given by the Greeks as a description of the shape of the tuberous roots; *orkhis* means testicle. And because of this resemblance orchids were said to be a powerful aphrodisiac, for man and beast. Further, men who ate orchid roots would begat male children. In medieval England, which was far more outspoken than we fancy ourselves to be today, the folk names for many of their wild orchids were slang words for testicles: dog stones, fooles stones, goat stones, sweet cods, soldier's cullions, etc. (Cullion, which also meant a low wretch or a "base fellow," came from the Latin *coleus*, or testicle.)

PRAIRIE WHITE FRINGED ORCHIS

Satyrion, another popular medieval word for orchids and still used in France for certain varieties, was derived from satyr, the name of the lustful wood deities of Greek mythology, and also refers obliquely to the shape of the tubers and their aphrodisiacal reputation.

Of the one hundred and forty wild orchids native to North America, our names by comparison have a picture-book ring: phantom orchis, snake-mouth, fairyslipper, whip-poor-will-shoe, moss nymph, bog-rose orchid, silver slipper, three-birds, moccasin-flower, twayblade, grass-pink, butterfly orchid, bee-swarm orchid, ARETHUSA, CALYPSO, LADIES'-TRESSES, LADY'S-SLIPPER, POGO-NIA, and RATTLESNAKE PLANTAIN.

June 9, 1854.—Find the great fringed orchis out apparently two or three days . . . a large spike of peculiarly delicate, pale purple flowers growing in the luxuriant and shady swamp. It is remarkable that this, one of the airiest of all our flowers, should also be one of the rarest, for the most part, not seen at all. . . . Only the skunk or owl, or other inhabitant of the swamp, beholds it. It does not pine because man does not admire it. I am inclined to think of it as a relic of the past, as much as the arrowhead or the tomahawk. —HENRY DAVID THOREAU, *Journals*

I remember once being asked if I had ever done any work to improve orchids. I stared at the questioner for a moment or two, fumbling for a reply. And then I said, perhaps a little impatiently: "Improve orchids? But who on earth would dream of wanting them improved?"—LUTHER BURBANK, 1846–1926, *The Harvest of the Years*

January, 1910. Oh, if only man brought his ingenuity to bear on protecting, not on destroying. . . . Were a miracle to produce in our woods some astounding orchid, a thousand hands would stretch out to tear it up, to destroy it . . . and then people are amazed that it is rare!—ANDRE GIDE, *Journals*

O R P I N E got its name by mistake, because of a family tie with the stonecrops (so called because of their preference for stony ground). A European stonecrop with yellow flowers was known in French as *orpiment,* which is the word for a yellow paint made from arsenic trisulphide, and orpiment comes directly from the Latin *auripigmentus,* "golden pigment." But there also was a European stonecrop of similar shape and structure that had red-dish-purple flowers. No matter. The golden name was passed along willy-nilly, though the concept of a purple-flowered *orpiment* is as contradictory in terms as a "red-headed blonde." The English word orpine is a contraction of the original French, *orpiment.*

The purple orpine that grows wild today throughout our eastern and mid-western states is the European original, first brought to this country as a garden flower. The purple flowers, by the way, are hard to come by; fields of orpine will grow year after year without a bud or blossom. Its oldest and most familiar nickname is live-forever, because orpine is a succulent—one of those fleshy plants that can store moisture—and it will survive long seasons of dry weather.

There were many superstitions connected with orpine, which may account for another early nickname—witches'-money. If you kept a pot of orpine in your house, and a witch, male or female, crossed your threshold, the orpine would instantly wither. And if a bunch of orpine were gathered on Midsummer's Eve and hung over your door, there would be no sickness or disease in the house as long as the leaves stayed green. From this association with Midsummer's Eve, there arose another old nickname for orpine—"midsummer-men." John Aubrey, an English antiquary and author of a book on folklore (1696), wrote: "I remember, the maids (especially the Cook maids and Dairymaids) would stick up in some chinks of the joists, etc. Midsummer-men, which are slips of Orpines. They placed them by pairs, one for such a man, the other for such a maid his sweet-heart, and accordingly as the Orpine did incline to, or recline from the other, that there would be love or aversion; if either did wither, death."

Pudding-bag plant was yet another early nickname, because the fleshy leaves are inflatable. Hold an orpine leaf in your mouth or gently work it between your fingers; the outer membrane will separate from the spine, and the leaf can be blown up like a small balloon, or a pudding-bag.

We have no plant so indestructible as garden orpine, or live-forever, which our grandmothers nursed and for which they are cursed by man and farmer. The fat, tender, succulent dooryard stripling turned out to be a monster that would devour the earth. I have seen acres of meadow land destroyed by it. . . . It lives by its stalk and leaf, more than by its root. . . . It laughs the plow, the hoe, the cultivator to scorn . . . —JOHN BURROUGHS, *A Year in the Fields*, 1897

The only bed of flowering Orpine I ever saw in America was in the millyard of Miller Rose at Kettle Hole—and a really lovely expanse of bloom it was, broken only by old worn millstones which formed the doorsteps. He told with pride that his grandmother planted it, and "it was the flowering variety that no one else had in Rhode Island, not even in the greenhouses in Newport." Miller Rose ground corn meal and flour with ancient millstones, and infinitely better were his grindings than "store meal." He was a famous preacher, having a pulpit built of heavy stones in the woods near his mill. A little trying it was to hear the outpourings of his long sermons on summer afternoons, while you waited for him to come down from his pulpit and prophesyings to give you your bag of meal. In sentimental association with his name, he had a few straggling Roses around his millyard, and, with Orpine, he could gather a very pretty posy for all who came to Kettle Hole.—ALICE MORSE EARLE, *Old Time Gardens*, 1901

O S W E G O   T E A. See BERGAMOT

P A S Q U E - F L O W E R—This is the paschal flower, because it usually blooms during the Easter and Passover holidays. *Pasque* was the Old French word for both these religious festivals;

paschal and *pasque* come from the Hebrew *pesakh,* a passing over.

There are some thirty varieties of pasque-flowers native to Japan, Siberia, the Near East, Europe, and our western states. The cup-shaped blooms can be red, yellow, white or lavender. In America, white and lavender are the usual colors, and a western nickname for the pasque-flower is prairie smoke, because of the gray filaments on the flower head when it has gone to seed.

These Pasque floures hath many small leaves finely cut or jagged, like those of Carrots: among which rise up naked stalkes, rough and hairie; whereupon do grow beautifull floures of a bright delayed purple colour. When the whole floure is past, ther succeedeth an head or knop of many gray hairy lockes . . . Ruellius writeth, that the Pasque floure groweth in France in untoiled places: in Germanie they grow in rough and stonie places, and oftentimes on rockes.

Those with purple floures do grow verie plentifully in the pasture or close belonging to the parsonage house of a small village six miles from Cambridge, called Hildersham: the Parsons name was Mr. Fuller, a very kind and loving man, and willing to shew unto any man the said close.—JOHN GERARD, *Herbal,* 1597

Prairie dogs are said to be very fond of the early flowers. This is a singular taste, and we may well wonder, if the report be correct, when we consider the bad reputation which the plant had in times gone by. An old writer speaks of it as follows: "The Herb, Flower, or Root being taken inwardly, are without doubt deleterious, or deadly: It kills by making the Patient look Laughing all the while. . . . By its Poisonous qualities it hurts the Senses and Understanding, thereby causing Foolishness; and Convulsing the Nerves, especially of the Mouth, Jaws, and Eyes, draws them this way and that way, making the sick seem to the by-standers as if he continually Laughed, whereas it is only a Convulsive Motion; and so the poor Patient, dying in this condition, the lookers-on think he dies Laughing, but he goes out of the world under the Sense of violent Convulsions . . ."—THOMAS MEEHAN, *The Native Flowers and Ferns of the United States,* 1880

Perhaps the farmers who did not want to move out of the Sand Counties had some deep reason, rooted far back in history, for preferring to stay. I am reminded of this every April when the pasque-flowers bloom on every gravelly ridge. Pasques do not say much, but I infer that their preference harks back to the glacier that put the gravel there. Only gravel ridges are poor enough to offer pasques full elbow-room in April sun. They endure snows, sleets, and bitter winds for the privilege of blooming alone.—ALDO LEOPOLD, *A Sand County Almanac,* 1949

PASSION FLOWER—The state flower of Tennessee and often known by the charming nickname of maypop, but not because it blooms in May. Maypop is the anglicization of the Indian *maracock,* as the Virginian tribes called it, the name having made its way from the Tupi Indians of South America, up through the Arawak and Carib tribes, and into North America. In the original Tupi, the name was *maraca-cui-iba*—the "rattle fruit"—because of the gourd-like fruits whose seeds rattle when the fruit is dried.

As for the taste of passion flower fruit, it depends on the variety.

PASSION FLOWER

Some are unedible and others so sweet they have become an important commercial crop, not only for the fruit but for flavorings and beverages. Captain John Smith, for example, described the "maracocks" he found in Virginia as "a pleasant wholesome fruit much like a lemon."

The name passion flower, or *flos passionis*, was given by the Spaniards, who found within the luscious tropical blooms a resemblance to the instruments of Christ's Passion. The leaf symbolizes the spear. The five anthers, the five wounds. The tendrils, the cords or whips. The column of the ovary, the pillar of the cross. The stamens, the hammers. The three styles, the three nails. The fleshy threads within the flower, the crown of thorns. The calyx, the glory or nimbus. The ten sepals and petals, the ten faithful apostles. (Peter denied Christ, Judas betrayed him; thus they were left out.)

> The Spanish Friers for some imaginarie resemblances in the floure, and in a counterfeit figure, by adding what was wanting, they made it as it were an Epitome of our Saviours Passion: thus superstitious persons always contrive an idle fancy. . . . In the West Indies, whereas it naturally growes, it beares a fruit, when it is ripe of the bignesse and colour of Pomegranates . . . the pulpe is whitish, and the liquor is somewhat tart: they open them as they do egges, and the liquor is supped off with great delight, both by the Indians and Spaniards, neither if they sup off many of them shall they find their stomach opprest. . . . It hath been brought into our English gardens, where it growes very well, but floures only in some few places, and in hot and seasonable yeares: it is in good plenty growing with Mistresse Tuggy at Westminster, where I have some yeares seen it beare a great many floures.—JOHN GERARD, *Herbal*, 1597

> I tried futiley to make jelly of our passion fruit, which sprawls its exquisite lacy vines all over the east grove through the late summer. . . . The fruit resembles a little the May apple, but is of an open, fibrous texture. There is a passion fruit liqueur that is the primary ingredient, after the varied rums, of that marvelous and deadly drink, the Zombie, and I was sure I had heard of passion fruit

jelly. . . . I gathered a skirtfull of the fruit and went home to my experiment. Perhaps I should have eliminated the skin or the seeds, but at any rate the exotic jelly on which I had set my heart did not materialize. The mixture jellied, but it tasted like a medieval poison, acrid, and strange, and I threw it out with horror.
—Marjorie Kinnan Rawlings, *Cross Creek*, 1942

The passion flower was formerly used as a nerve sedative to allay general restlessness, to relieve insomnia, and in the relief of certain types of convulsions and spasmodic disorders. It was also attributed with anodyne properties and used in the treatment of various neuralgias.—*Dispensatory of the United States*, 1950

P E N N Y R O Y A L—There are several American mints known as pennyroyal. The name was borrowed from a European herb, the true pennyroyal of ancient repute. The Latin word for it was *puleium regium,* or "fleabane royal"—a sovereign remedy for dispelling fleas and other such pediculi. *Puleium* came from *pulex,* or flea, also the root for *puce,* the French word for flea. The color puce, a sort of reddish-gray, first became fashionable at the French court and was given its name, in one of those flights of stylish fancies, because it was the same shade as the blood of a flea. (Fleas, we must remember, played a far more intimate role in high society in those days than they do now.) The European mint that was helpful in warding off pediculi came to England with the Normans as *puliol* royal and sifted into modern English as pennyroyal.

As early as 1000 A.D., pennyroyal smelling salts were found to be efficacious against seasickness. A garland of pennyroyal worn round the brow was a "great force against the swimming of the head, the paine and giddinesse thereof." A few drops of oil of pennyroyal with sugar used to be given for whooping cough. The Indians used the American varieties for much the same complaints—as a "smelling weed" and a tea to relieve headaches, as an insect repellent, and as a cure for fevers and spasms. It's still used in commercial mosquito repellents and presumably will discourage fleas, too, just as it did in the old days.

And now I am upon the subject of Insects, it may not be impro-
per to mention some few Remedies against those that are most
Vexatious in this Climate. There are two Sorts without Doors, that
are great Nuisances, the Tikes [ticks] and the Horse Flies. . . .
Both these sorts are apt to be troublesome during the Warm Season, but have such an aversion to Penny Royal, that they will attack
no Part that is rubb'd with the Juice of that fragrant Vegetable.
And a Strong Decoction of this is likewise the most effectual
Remedy against Seed-tikes, which bury themselves in your Legs.
—WILLIAM BYRD, *Histories of the Dividing Line betwixt Virginia
and North Carolina,* 1728

We went down to the edge of short grass above some rocky cliffs
where the deep sea broke with a great noise, though the wind was
down and the water looked quiet a little way from shore. Among
the grass grew such pennyroyal as the rest of the world could not
provide. There was a fine fragrance in the air as we gathered it
sprig by sprig and stepped along carefully, and Mrs. Todd pressed
her aromatic nosegay between her hands and offered it to me again
and again. "There's nothin' like it," she said; "Oh, no, there's no
such pennyr'yal as this in the state of Maine. It's the right pattern
of the plant, and all the rest I ever see is but an imitation. . ."
—SARAH ORNE JEWETT, *The Country of the Pointed Firs,* 1896

P E N T S T E M O N—The Greek name was given by
Linnaeus when he classified the plants of the world, and it means,
very simply, "five stamens." The fifth stamen is bearded, hence
the nickname "beard-tongue;" other pretty names for various of
the pentstemons are: pride of the mountains, scarlet trumpet,
prairie fire, foxglove pentstemon, azure pentstemon, rose elf. But
just how many pentstemons are there? The list gets longer and
longer as the years go by. The first few Eastern pentstemons were
known in colonial days, and as explorers and settlers headed west,
more and more varieties were discovered, since the pentstemons
are largely a western species. The top number classified in the
1880's was seventy. By 1922, one hundred and fifty varieties were

LARGE-FLOWERED PENTSTEMON

known, according to the Britannica. By 1960, H. W. Rickett of the New York Botanical Garden wrote that there were more than two hundred varieties throughout America. Who knows? There may still be more, even today, waiting to be discovered.

A ramble down a mountain stream in the Sierras affords a succession of most delightful surprises. Willow copses, alternating with tangles of larkspur, fireweed, and monk's-hood, are followed by open, velvety meadows, starred by blue and white daisies, or diversified by the pure spikes of the milk-white rein orchis, or the lovely blossoms of the pink monkey-faces; while further down, the stream perchance suddenly narrows and deepens, flowing by some jutting rock-wall resplendent with crimson pentstemons. . . —MARY ELIZABETH PARSONS, *Wild Flowers of California*, 1900

Next year, sans faut, I shall go exploring into the hinterlands of the Penstemon world, cross the civilized frontiers and push on into that wilderness of new kinds our plant explorers have been turning up in the Rockies. The Penstemons are as American in origin as Phlox, and yet the average gardener knows little of this great and interesting family. Here and there a western catalogue offers a few new names. What fun to explore that family in its ramifications! I've no illusions about all of the Penstemons being beauties, yet the experience will be worth the trouble.—RICHARDSON WRIGHT, *The Gardener's Bed-Book*, 1939

PERIWINKLE was not considered a wildflower until recently. An escapee, yes, but not prevalent enough to be officially listed, although it's been out of bounds for years and spreads lavishly on the shady ground it favors. In fact, periwinkle, in two of my wildflower guides, is not even listed as an import, so abundant has it become. But it's another of the Mediterranean plants that came to America by way of England.

The Latin name was *pervinca*, from *vincire*, to bind or entwine, because of the long winding, twining tendrils and rootlets. The Middle English name for it was *pervenke*, and from there it was modified to periwinkle. Now, as for the other periwinkle—the marine snail—its name came from *pina*, the Latin name for a certain variety of mussel, and *wincel*, the Old English for snail shell. Thus it was known as the *pinewincle*, and as the twists and turns of language go, both the plant and the snail wound up with the same name, though the sources of their names are utterly unrelated.

Myrtle is a purely American name for periwinkle and the one in most common use. The true myrtle is an evergreen European shrub with fragrant blue or pink flowers, and the name has no known meaning. The Romans called it *myrtillus*, the Greeks *myrtos*, and the Persians *murd*. This is the plant that symbolized immortality in the ancient world and was woven into wreathes to crown the winners of the Olympic games; it should not be confused with our "myrtle."

> Venus owns this herb, and saith that the leaves eaten by man and wife together, cause love between them.—DR. NICHOLAS CULPEPER, *English Physician and Complete Herbal*, 1649

> The Periwinkle—Ground Myrtle, we used to call it—was one of the most mysterious and elusive flowers I knew, and other children thus regarded it; but I had a deep affection for its lovely blue stars and clean, glossy leaves, a special love, since it was the first flower I saw blooming out of doors after a severe illness, and it seemed to welcome me back to life. . . . Everywhere it is a flower of mystery; it is the "Violette des Sorciers" of the French. Sadder is its Tuscan

name, "Flower of death," for it is used there as garlands at the burial of children; and is often planted on graves, just as it is here. A far happier folk-name was Joy-of-the-ground.—ALICE MORSE EARLE, *Old Time Gardens*, 1901

How could I forget Periwinkle! Periwinkle that opens a brave blue eye upon the very dawn of the year and often gives an azure wink just outside the gate of winter. I would no more have a garden without a lot of Periwinkle than I would without a lot of Daffodils. If you have a woodland path or a half-shaded border, line it thickly with the little white early Violet; behind these wind a ribbon of Periwinkle; and behind these still make a riot of pale star Daffodils. What matter the stock market with a spring so wealthily caparisoned?—LOUISE BEEBE WILDER, *What Happens in My Garden*, 1935

P H A C E L I A—There are close to two hundred flowers in this group, native to the Andes and to North America. The name was given in the early 1700's by Antoine de Jussieu, a professor at the Jardin des Plantes, Paris, where the rare and the beautiful were often sent by flower-hunters who ranged the world. The name came from the Greek *phakelos,* or bundle, because the flowers are clustered, or bundled, at the top of the stalk. *Phakelos* is also the root for the Roman *fasces,* bundles of rods bound together with an ax, which was the emblem of authority for Roman magistrates. *Fasces* in turn was the root word for Fascism.

Phacelia is one of the few scientific plant names in common usage, although there are local nicknames for various species: baby-eyes, bluebells, mistmaiden, waterleaf (origin uncertain), wild heliotrope (from the Greek *helio,* sun, and *trope,* to turn— that is, it turns toward the sun), and scorpionweed. This last name was given because the flower stalk of this variety of phacelia curves up and over like a scorpion's tail; in botanic lingo this is known as a "scorpioid" curve, and a similar nickname was given to FORGET-ME-NOTS for the same reason.

Possibly the loveliest of all in this family is the white fringed phacelia of the southern mountains where masses of it cover the woodland floor in April and May. These particular phacelias, each blossom like porcelain lace, were found by André Michaux, a French farmer turned naturalist, who had already traveled through the Tigris and Euphrates valleys and enjoyed such adventures as curing the Shah of Persia from a mysterious wasting disease, and, on another occasion, being robbed and turned naked into the desert by Arab brigands. In America, from 1785 to 1796, Michaux explored "Les wilderness," as he called it—an incredible stretch of unknown territory, from the Bahamas, through Florida and the Cherokee nation, the Great Smokies, the Great Craggies, up the Appalachian chain, into Canada to Lake Mistassini, and out to southern Illinois. He died on an expedition into the mountains of Madagascar in 1802.

> *The Phacelia for Bouquets.*—The Phacelia works up beautifully in bouquets. Everybody admired these flowers; many a time this summer have I cut a Pink and a cluster of those delicate flowers for button-hole bouquets, and every time they called forth pleasant remarks. If there is any thing prettier than Phacelia for bouquets, I should like to know it.— Mrs. E.P.W., Canandaigua, Michigan, *Vick's Monthly Magazine*, March, 1878

P H L O X—Apart from a variety that grows in Siberia, phlox are an American flower of some seventy different species. The name was an ancient one that Pliny used in reference to a flame-red CAMPION, or catchfly, so named because *phlox* means fire in Greek. It comes from the verb *phlegein*, to burn, which is also the root word for phlegm, believed in ancient medicine to be the cause, rather than the companion, of inflaming fevers and sore throats, etc. Linnaeus took the old name of phlox away from the red campion and gave it to the American flowers, some say because the buds furl to a point like little torches or flames, but his reason has never been made clear.

Most phlox of the eastern United States were known by the

end of the 1700's, and plants had been sent to Europe—such as the wild blue phlox of early spring that are often known as wild-sweet-william. (They should not be confused with the garden variety of sweet william, which comes from Eurasia and according to tradition was given its English name in honor of William the Conqueror.)

But America was a continent of continuing floral surprises. Michaux (see under PHACELIA) found a new creeping phlox in the North Carolina mountains. David Douglas, the Scottish naturalist (see under MARIPOSA), found numerous others in his westward wanderings. And in Texas in 1835, James Drummond, another intrepid Scot, found the phlox that has been credited with being the ancestor of most of our loveliest garden varieties. Drummond had been sent to explore for plants by the Glasgow Botanical Society. Here is an account of one leg of his travels, told by Sir John Richardson, also a Scottish naturalist and an arctic explorer: "Mr. Drummond in his excursions over the Rocky Mountains, had frequent opportunities of observing the manners of the grizzly bears, and it often happened that in turning the point of a rock or sharp angle of a valley he came suddenly upon one or more of them. On such occasions they reared on their hind-legs, and made a loud noise like a person breathing quick, but much harsher. He kept his ground, without attempting to molest them; and they on their part, after attentively regarding him for some time, generally wheeled round and galloped off. When he discovered them from a distance, he generally frightened them away by beating on a large tin-box in which he carried his specimens of plants. . ."

After his American adventures, Drummond went on to Cuba to botanize and there died of fever. But the crimson phlox that he had collected in Texas had already been received in Glasgow, and the Botanical Society gave the new plant his name—*Phlox drummondii*—"that it may serve as a frequent memento of its unfortunate discoverer."

Phlox drummondii. A bed of this plant has hardly yet been seen;

for it is far too precious and uncommon to be possessed by anyone, except in small quantities; but I have had such a bed described to me, and I can readily believe that it produced all the brilliancy that my informant represented.—JOHN LINDLEY, *Botanical Register*, London, 1837

Many of the individual blossoms of my Phloxes are larger than a fifty-cent piece; a number of them are larger by measurement than a silver dollar. Always erect, neat and smiling, never needing to be staked, when once grown they must always be dear to a gardener's heart. By breaking off the heads of Phlox immediately after blooming a second crop of flowers will appear in about three weeks. The heads will not be so large as the first, but they will amply repay the slight trouble.—HELENA RUTHERFURD ELY, *A Woman's Hardy Garden*, 1907

Of plants that grow in low-spreading masses several species of the Phlox are most desirable. Moss-pink, the little evergreen with lavender-colored flowers, together with the white and many other varieties, are all charming subjects. How gracefully, too, the moss-pink drapes a grave, paying its lovely but voiceless tribute to the departed!

Latter midsummer and early fall bring a fresh color-surprise to the garden. It is the season of the hybridized Phlox. . . . America furnished them, Europe has hybridized them. These glowing shades of salmon, rose, and vermillion, together with the numerous pure white and creamy-white varieties, are the more striking from the grand flower-trusses and the tall stalks upon which they are placed. The Phlox, however, like numerous other florists' flowers, is not without crying colors, its purples and rose-purples in particular being generally objectionable.—GEORGE H. ELLWANGER, *The Garden's Story*, 1889

The Widow Slater dressed always in a Victorian white shirtwaist and a long full-flowing black skirt. She trailed her long black skirts through the puddles of soapsuds splashed around her and carried great dripping armfuls of half-wrung sheets to the clothes line, and was concerned, not with the hardships, but the weather and the phlox. The weather almost always suited her, for if it was fine the clothes would dry well, and if it rained, why, nothing was better for bleaching them. The phlox bothered her for the reason that they grew wild in the yard around the wash-bench and she was afraid of stepping on them. "They look up at you with little faces," she said, "and it seems treacherous to stomp them."—MARJORIE KINNAN RAWLINGS, *Cross Creek*, 1942

P I C K E R E L W E E D—Big arrow-shaped leaves, a tall stalk of blue flowers, and one of a kind, native to North American fresh water shallows. The name "pickerel weed" came from England, where it had been used for centuries for a similar type of pond-weed with large leaves and white or reddish flowers on a long stalk. And why pickerel weed, specifically? Because of an ancient biological belief in "spontaneous generation." For example, there were certain barnacles that generated geese; there were certain trees, sworn to by travelers, that blossomed with sheep; and there were certain water weeds that spontaneously bred pike and pickerel. Izaak Walton discussed this age-old curiosity; the "learned Gesner" of whom he speaks was the author of *Historia Animalium* (1558).

Piscator. The mighty Pike is taken to be the Tyrant (as the Salmon is the King) of the fresh waters. 'Tis not to be doubted, but that they are bred, some by generation, and some not: as namely, of a Weed called *Pickerel-weed*, unless learned Gesner be much mistaken, for he says, this weed and other glutinous matter, with the help of the Sun's heat in some particular Months, and some Ponds apted for it by nature, do become Pikes. . . . for they have observed that where none have been put into Ponds, yet they have there found many; and that there has been plenty of that weed in those Ponds, and that that weed both breeds and feeds them . . . —IZAAK WALTON, *The Compleat Angler*, 1653

Along the Saranac River in the Adirondacks a few days ago I found the pickerel weed more fully and luxuriantly in bloom than on any previous occasion. The slender spikes of delicate blue flowers reared themselves above great beds of polished leaves, making a rich border to the winding river. Our guide told us that in spring the pickerel laid their eggs among these plants, which at that season are not visible above the water, and that later the moose fed upon their leaves.—FRANCES THEODORA PARSON, *According to the Seasons*, 1902

PIMPERNEL—This is a European family of plants with only one variety growing wild in America—the scarlet pimpernel, whose small flowers are vermillion-orange with purple hearts. The name is believed to come from the Latin *piperinella*, or "little peppers," because the fine, round, bullet-like seeds of the pimpernels resemble pepper seeds. An old nickname still common both in England and America is "poor man's weather glass." When the flowers are open, there's fair weather ahead; when the flowers are shut, wet weather is on the way.

Peach is full of old shepherd lore . . . For rain he says, "Crickets will sing sharply, and swallows fly low." Also that toads will walk out across the road, and frogs will change from green to brown. Also the Scarlet Pimpernel will close her eyes.—J. R. ANDERSON, *Garden Book*, 1768

"The Scarlet Pimpernel?" said Suzanne, with a merry laugh. "What a droll name! What is the Scarlet Pimpernel, Monieur?"
She looked at Sir Andrew with eager curiosity. The young man's face had become almost transfigured. His eyes shone with admiration for his leader. "The Scarlet Pimpernel, Mademoiselle, is the name of a humble English wayside flower; but it is also the name chosen to hide the identity of the best and bravest man in all the world."
Here interposed the young Vicomte, "I have heard speak of this Scarlet Pimpernel. A little flower—red?—yes! They say that every time a royalist escapes to England, that devil, the Public Prosecutor, receives in Paris a paper with the little flower dessinated in red upon it."—BARONESS EMMUSKA ORCZY, *The Scarlet Pimpernel*, 1905

PINXTERBLOOM. See under AZALEA

PIPSISSEWA—This is an Indian word. In the language of the Cree, it was *pipisisikweu*, meaning "it breaks it into small pieces." That is to say, the juice of the plant breaks down kidney stones or gallstones. This Indian remedy was passed along to the white man, and indeed a tonic extract from pipsissewa was used in pharmaceutics until quite recently. It was still listed as a diuretic in the 1940's.

Prince's pine is another name. I've also seen it catalogued in old books as prince's pride, but have not been able to discover the significance of either nickname. Pipsissewa belongs to the wintergreen family and has the typical wintergreen flowers—waxy, nodding blossoms that are doubly beautiful under a magnifying glass.

June 13, 1854. The little globular, dropping, reddish buds of the pipsissewa are now very pretty.

July 3, 1852. The pipsissewa must have been in blossom some time. The back side of its petal, "cream-colored, tinged with purple," which is turned toward the beholder, while the face is toward the earth, is the handsomer . . . a very pretty little chandelier of a flower, fit to adorn the forest floors. Its buds are nearly as handsome. —HENRY DAVID THOREAU, *Journals*

The prince's pine is a charming little plant, and may be found beneath the undergrowth in the great coniferous woods of the Sierras, where it sits demurely with bowed head, like some cloistered nun engaged with her own meditations. It has an exquisite perfume, like that of the lily of the valley. The common prince's pine of the Eastern States is more rare with us . . . a more vigorous plant, with four to seven purplish flowers in the cluster, while its leaves are never spotted.—MARY ELIZABETH PARSONS, *Wild Flowers of California*, 1900

Pipsissewa—Parts Used: Leaves. Do take it easy on this pretty little plant—it's not terribly common. The leaves make a pleasant nibble with their wintergreen taste. A tea can be made of the leaves by steeping them in hot water for 8 minutes.—ADRIENNE CROWHURST, The *Weed Cookbook*, 1972

PLANTAIN—This is not to be confused with robin's plantain, the small blue daisy-like flower that blooms in early spring when the robins come north. Nor with rattlesnake plantain, one of our native orchids. Nor with the plantain of the tropics, a member of the banana family. The true plantains are a family unto themselves—all two hundred and seventy of them now thriving on this planet. I particularly have in mind the two ineradicable plantains that infest our lawns and gardens: the common or great plantain, and the so-called English plantain, both of which are wind-pollinated—one breath of air and their stock is doubled. And both are aliens introduced from Europe, presumably by mistake. They've always had a reputation for being troublesome weeds.

The Romans called this family the *plantago*, from *planta*, meaning broad or spreading, which was the root word for "plant" and also meant the sole of the foot. *Plantago* was anglicized to plantain. By curious coincidence, the Indian's name for the plantains was "white man's foot."

Plantains were once used in medicine, for ulcers, nausea, ear aches, and so forth, but their reputation began to fade in the 1800's, although *The Farmer's Encyclopaedia* (1852) noted: "The genus in general is mucilaginous and somewhat astringent, qualities which render it not altogether a useless rustic medicine." And further, "Cows and horses do not relish this plant, but it is eaten by sheep, goats, and swine." The opinion of cows and horses notwithstanding, plantain can be eaten as a spring green, and contemporary wild food cookbooks recommend it—the young leaves chopped in salad or soup or boiled like spinach.

Strangely enough, of all the listings in this book, plantain is one that has been immortalized left and right in poetry.

> Mother of worts,
> Over thee carts creaked,
> Over thee Queens rode,
> Over thee brides bridalled,
> Over thee bulls breathed,
> All these thou withstoodst,

Venom and vile things,
And all the loathly things,
That through the land rove.
                    —AELFRIC, c. 955–c. 1020,
                    Lacunga

Whereso'er they tread, beneath them
Springs a flower unknown among us;
Springs the White Man's Foot in blossom.
                    —HENRY WADSWORTH LONGFELLOW,
                    Hiawatha, 1855

Knot-grass, plantain—all the social weeds,
Man's mute companions, following where he leads.
                    —OLIVER WENDELL HOLMES, 1809–1894,
                    The Island Ruin

P L E U R I S Y - R O O T. See BUTTERFLY WEED

P O G O N I A—The name was given in the early 1700's
by Professor Antoine de Jussieu, of the Jardin des Plantes, Paris—
the botanist who also named the phacelia. Again, his choice came
from Greek: pogonia from *pogon,* or beard, because of the fringed
lower lip of the flower. The jutting, open angle of this lower lip
probably accounts for the rose pogonia's occasional nicknames,
"snake-mouth" and "adder's-mouth." It is the rosiest of pinks,
with a scent that has been compared to violets or ripe raspberries—
although Thoreau wrote that the pogonia had a "snaky odor."

There is also a whorled pogonia, named for the whorl of leaves
like a ruffed green collar on the neck of the plant. Its flower is
surrealistic, a science fiction flower from another planet—greenish-
yellow with three long madder-purple sepals, one pointing up like
the horn of a unicorn, the other two pointing down like elephant
tusks. Pogonias are members of the orchid family and closely
related to the ARETHUSA. The Dr. Barton mentioned below is
Benjamin Smith Barton, a Philadelphia physician and naturalist,

WHORLED POGONIA

who wrote *Elements of Botany* (1803), the first basic botany by an American.

Dr. Barton's conscientious attempts at description delight me, and in this case, his "peach-blossom red" would probably satisfy most masculine admirers of the Pogonia. To the yellow bearded lip that makes the Arethusa so bright, it adds a pretty tuft of purple-pink, and if the Arethusa is striking in its appearance, this Pogonia is to be praised for its refinement. I have seen specimens of this Pogonia from Japan, and should think it would appeal strongly to the native artists as a subject, but as yet I have not recognized it on any vase or fan.—HENRY BALDWIN, *The Orchids of New England*, 1884

Rose-Pogonia: It grows generally in bogs, among sphagnum and sedges, and in places so wet that those who go out collecting in patent-leather shoes have generally to be satisfied with admiring from a distance. Sometimes a bog will be perfectly ablaze with the bright blossoms, and we have frequently seen this beautiful sight, especially in the State of New Jersey.—THOMAS MEEHAN, *The Native Flowers and Ferns of the United States*, 1880

My friend of the meadow and wildwood had gathered that morning a glorious harvest, over two thousand stems of Pogonia, from his own hidden spot, which he has known for forty years and from whence no other hand ever gathers. For a little handful of these flower heads he easily obtains a dollar. It is not easily earned money to stand in heavy rubber boots in marsh mud and water reaching nearly to the waist, but it is happy work. Jeered at in his early life by fools for his wood-roving tastes, he has now the pleasure and honor of supplying wild flowers to our public schools, and being the authority to whom scholars and teachers refer in vexed questions of botany.—ALICE MORSE EARLE, *Old Time Gardens*, 1901

P O K E W E E D—At first glance, this looks like an everyday, descriptive sort of name, pure and simple. It pokes up out of the ground, bigger and taller than any other sprouts around it and pokes along until it has grown as high as a bush—big branchy leaves, a red stalk, and racemes of little white flowers followed by dark purple juicy berries, which the birds love. Pigeon-berry is an old nickname from the days before our passenger pigeons were wiped out; the berries had been one of their favorites, too.

The name pokeweed, however, in spite of its apparent simplicity, comes from the Virginian Indian *pokan*, which meant any red-juiced plant used as a stain or dye. *Pokan* came from *pak*, which meant blood. (Puccoon, from the same source, was an early word for BLOODROOT.) In Indian medicine, a pokeweed poultice was used for cancers, scrofula, the "itch," and rheumatism, and in small doses for syphilis.

During Polk's presidential campaign (1845) pokeweed twigs were worn by his followers, and later it was said that the plant had got its name from the President. But pokeweed had been pokeweed long before James Knox Polk arrived on the political scene. Another nickname for this American plant is inkberry.

The Pokeweed . . . When the juice of its berries is put upon paper or the like, it dyes it a deep purple, which is as fine as any in the world, and it is a pity that no method has as yet been discovered of making this color last on woolen and linen cloth, for it fades very soon. Mr. Bartram mentioned that having hit his foot against a stone, he had gotten a violent pain in it; that he then bethought himself of putting a leaf of the pokeweed on his foot, by which he had lost the pain in a short time. . . . The English and several Swedes make use of the leaves in spring, when they just come out and are still tender and soft, and eat them, partly in the manner we eat spinach. . . . Great care has to be taken, for if you eat the plant when it is large and its leaves are no longer soft, you may expect death as a consequence, a calamity which seldom fails to follow, for the plant has then got a power of purging the body to excess.—Peter Kalm, *Travels into North America*, 1748–1751

Pokeweed is a native American, and what a lusty, royal plant it is! It never invades cultivated fields, but hovers about the borders and looks over the fences like a painted Indian sachem. Thoreau coveted its strong purple stalk for a cane, and the robins eat its dark crimson-juiced berries.—John Burroughs, *A Bunch of Herbs*, 1881

I hunt through the grove after a spring rain, basket in hand, for the most tender shoots, cutting those from six to eight inches in length. I trim off the leaves and thin skin and cook the shoots exactly as I do asparagus, serving them on buttered toast with a rich cream sauce poured over, and strips of crisp breakfast bacon around them. The flavor is delicate and delicious, with a faint taste of iron.—Marjorie Kinnan Rawlings, *Cross Creek*, 1942

POINSETTIA. See Spurge

POLARPLANT. See Compass Plant

POLYGALA—Gaywings, bird-on-the-wing, and flowering wintergreen are nicknames, but polygala or "fringed polygala" is as commonly used, although it's the botanic designation. The name goes back to the Greeks—*poly*, much, and *gala*, milk, because the polygalas of the Old World were reputed to induce the flow of milk in nursing mothers. (*Gala* is also the root word for our sun's galaxy, the milky way.)

Milkwort became the general English term for this worldwide family of plants, some five hundred strong, found everywhere but in the polar regions and New Zealand. Our typical American milkworts have tiny flowers crowded in cloverlike heads. The fringed polygala looks utterly unrelated and is often mistaken for an orchid, which is perhaps the reason that it's rarely spoken of as milkwort, that name being reserved for the less glamorous members of the family. Polygala may mean the same thing, but it has a more elegant ring to it.

The stroller in the moist May woods will well remember those mauve-winged blooms among the moss that seems to flutter in the breeze, like a brood of tiny purple butterflies with fringy tails, or in a sheltered nook appear to have settled in a swarm among the winter-green leaves. . . . It is one of our oddest and prettiest spring flowers; in its very singular shape quite suggesting an orchid, with its two spreading petals and deep lavender-colored tasselled sleeve. But indeed, it has long been laughing at us in that sleeve, as we have brought away its flowers from the woods. . .

The polygala found out long ago that some means must be adopted to keep its foothold in the woods, so it formed a little plan to anchor itself in its home beyond the reach of bouquet hunters, offering one posy for the boutonniere, and another for mother earth. . . . These pale, pouch-like underground flowers are not beautiful to look at, but they plant the mould with seeds every year, and thus perpetuate the purple beds of bloom.—WILLIAM HAMILTON GIBSON, *Sharp Eyes*, 1892

P R I M R O S E—The root word is Latin: *primus,* or first, because these are among the first flowers of spring. Thus they were known as *primulas,* a diminutive of *primus* and roughly meaning "the little firstling." In Old French and Middle English *primula* become *primerole,* and then slipped into primrose, influenced by the idea of its being the first "rose," or flower, of the spring season. Curiously, in today's French, the primrose is *la primevère,* and *primerose* means hollyhock. (In English, *that* means "holy mallow.")

This is an enormous family of plants, subdivided again and again by botanists. Variations of the classic primrose, commonly known in England as the COWSLIP, bloom in the Arctic, the Himalayas, the Mediterranean region, and the United States. Other members of the *primula* family that grow wild in America are bird's-eye primrose, Sierra primrose, starflower, shooting-star, LOOSESTRIFE, and PIMPERNEL.

Our evening primroses, however, are another genus altogether —the *Oenothera*, as Linnaeus named them, from the Greek *oinos*, wine, and *thera*, pursuing or imbibing, presumably because an allied European plant was thought to induce a thirst for wine. The *Oenothera* are almost exclusively North American, with a few Caribbean and South American species. The primrose name was given to them in the early 1600's by John Parkinson, the English herbalist, who was the first to describe these night-blooming flowers from the New World. Their scent reminded Parkinson of the wild primroses in English meadows, so he named the American flower "the tree primrose of Virginia." Apparently he was describing our tall, common, evening primrose that often grows to five feet in height. At any rate, the primrose name stuck, ever after. Among the handsomest of our native varieties is the glade lily or Missouri primrose, a low, creeping plant with yellow blossoms that are often six inches across. All evening primroses open suddenly with a quick nervous motion that not only can be seen, but sometimes even heard. At dawn, the blossoms fade.

Primula. If one takes his alpenstock in hand and climbs to the snow-line, he is apt to be rewarded by the charming flowers of the Sierra primrose. The little plants grow in the drip of the snow-banks, where the melting ice gradually liberates the tufts of ever-green leaves. The glowing flowers look as though they might have caught and held the last rosy reflections of the sunset upon the snow above them.—MARY ELIZABETH PARSONS, *Wild Flowers of California*, 1900

Oenothera. Can we really claim to know our evening primrose? Night after night, for weeks, its pale blooms have opened, and shed abroad their sweet perfume in the darkness in every glen and by every road-side; and yet how few of us have ever stopped to witness that beautiful impatience of the swelling bud, the eager bursting of its bounds, and the magic unfolding of the crinkly yellow petals?

But it is not to the primrose of the twilight, nor the opening bud nor fresh-perfumed flower, that I would now invite attention. . . . Go out now in the hot, sunny noon-time, and stroll among your withered primroses. Last night, when its four green sepals released their bright, glossy petals, a small moth quickly caught the signal. Its wings were of the purest rose-pink, bordered with yellow.

All through the night it fluttered among the fresh opening flowers, one of a countless host of feathery nocturnal moths and "millers." But as the sunrise has stolen upon these primroses, the fickle broods have all forgotten the flowers and dispersed afar. "All," did I say? Oh no; not all. Let us turn to our withered blossoms, and, one by one, look within their bells. Here is a bell that appears to have an extra petal folded within its throat; and upon opening the folds, we disclose our faithful nursling with pink and yellow wings; the earliest twilight sipper, that even on the approach of dawn is loth to leave the flower, and creeps into the wilting bloom, where it remains concealed through the following day. . . . These pretty moths are by no means rare. I once found three upon the same plant. Look, then, to your daylight primrose.—WILLIAM HAMILTON GIBSON, *Sharp Eyes*, 1892

Among the flowers great-aunt Lancilla loved most were evening primroses. I have never since then seen a large border, as she had, entirely given to them. She used to pick the flowers to float in finger bowls at dinner.—ELEANOUR SINCLAIR RHODE, *The Scented Garden*, 1931

PRINCE'S PINE. See PIPSISSEWA

PURSLANE—This is one of the most complicated of plant names to unravel because it's a combination of the name of the genus, to which purslanes belong, and an ancient pun in street Latin. What's more, purslane criss-crosses along the way with sea-shells and Chinese porcelains.

Let's begin with the botanic name, which is portulaca, a Latin word given to this genus in ages past. Etymologists are not agreed on its meaning. Some say there is none. Others suggest that it may mean "the milk-carrier," from *porto* and *lac,* because of the juicy leaves and stems that typify this family of plants. Still others suggest that it comes from *portula,* a little gate, because of the gate-like cover to the seed capsules. But whatever the meaning, portulaca it is, and ever more shall be.

Now to our Latin pun. In Roman times, the slang word for the vulva was *porca,* or sow, and in those ancient days the purslane-portulaca was used in medicine for uterine complaints. And here's where the Romans made their pun, a little play on words between *porca* and portulaca, and they came up with *porcillaca* as a nickname for the "womb-herb." *Porcillaca* moved into Italian as *porcellana,* into Old French as *porcelaine,* and eventually into English as purslane—meanwhile bringing along with it the official name, portulaca.

As I said earlier, purslane crossed paths with sea-shells and Chinese porcelains in its etymological wanderings. Let's drop back to the Roman slang, *porca.* This was also the source word for *porcella,* the little sow, or little vulva, as the Romans named the cowrie shell, because of its appearance. (A similar anatomic reference was used in Old Danish.) *Porcella,* traveling the same language route as purslane, went into Italian as *porcellana* and into Old French as *porcelaine.* When the first translucent Chinese ceramics were introduced to Europe, they too were named porcelain, because the fine glaze was like the sheen of the cowrie.

The purslane that is so common in America was originally a native of India, brought to Europe and from Europe to the New World, both as a vegetable and a medicinal herb. This particular variety, with small yellow flowers that open on sunny mornings, is the *Portulaca oleracea,* and *oleracea* is a Latin word for pot-herb. It had already run wild in the late 1700's, and the Reverend Manasseh Cutler of Boston listed purslane as a vegetable "naturally growing in this part of America . . . in cornfields . . . and esteemed by some as little inferior to asparagus." But somewhere along the line, it lost its reputation as a delicious green food, fell into disrepute as an insidious weed, and picked up the unattractive nickname of "pusley."

Our native milk-purslane, purslane speedwell, water-purslane, and sea-purslane are not related. The name was handed on to them by early settlers because of a similarity in form. The botanic name, portulaca, is now popularly used for the garden species native to Brazil.

Another enemy had come into the strawberries. . . . I refer, of course, to the greatest enemy of mankind, "pusley." The ground was carpeted with it . . . a fat, ground-clinging, spreading, greasy thing, and the most propagatious (it is not my fault if the word is not in the dictionary) plant I know. I saw a Chinaman, who came over with a returned missionary, and pretended to be converted, boil a lot of it in a pot, stir in eggs, and mix and eat in with relish. . .
—Charles Dudley Warner, *My Summer in a Garden*, 1870

As for purslane, this succulent plant has been eaten and appreciated in India and Persia for more than two thousand years. It is today a prized garden vegetable over much of Europe and Asia. . . . Just seeing the specific name of this plant, *oleraccea*, should indicate that here is savory food. The entire plant, stem, leaf and flower bud is good to eat. . . . Let's stop considering purslane worthless merely because it is so abundant and easily procured. Maybe purslane proves there is truth in the old cliché that states that "the best things in life are free."—Euell Gibbons, *Stalking the Wild Asparagus*, 1962

P Y R O L A is the ancient Latin name for this family of circumpolar plants that grow in the Arctic tundra and in cool northerly woods across America, Iceland, Great Britain, Scandinavia, and Siberia.

It was given because of the resemblance between the plant's leaves and the leaves of the pear tree, or *pirus*, and pyrola is the diminutive—"the little pear tree." This botanic title was picked up throughout Europe, and when Linnaeus was classifying, naming, and re-naming in the 1700's, he approved the choice and kept pyrola on his list.

Shinleaf, an old rural English nickname and still in common use, was given because the leaves were used as shin-plasters, another old English nickname for a poultice applied to a bruise. In Indian medicine our pyrolas, or shinleaf, were used for rheumatism, coughs, and cankers. These remedies were also used by the colonists, who then gave the plants their American nicknames—Indian lettuce and canker lettuce.

The waxy flowers, white, pink, or white with green veining, are strung along their stalks in much the same pattern as lily-of-the-valley—like miniature porcelain lampshades, and their long styles like miniature light-pulls.

In early spring, it is often the only living green thing among the dead tree leaves of the previous autumn, and serves admirably well to relieve the monotonous brown color of the forests, where it loves to dwell.—THOMAS MEEHAN, *The Native Flowers and Ferns of the United States*, 1880

A trip to the Sierras in August will yield many a prize to the flower-lover. Pyrolas, with waxen clusters, vie with Pipsissiwas. . . . A ramble in the woods one day brought us to the brink of a charming stream whose pure, ice-cold waters babbled along most invitingly. Following its course, we found ourselves in a delightfully cool, moist thicket, where, nestling in the deep shade, we found the beautiful, rich, glossy leaves of *Pyrola rotundifolia*. The leaves are roundish, of a beautiful bright, chrome green, highly polished, and the delicate flowers are rose-pink. . . . These pretty plants are called "shinleaf."—MARY ELIZABETH PARSONS, *Wild Flowers of California*, 1900

P Y X I E, the small creeping plant whose flowers range in color from rose-lilac to white. What more appropriate name, so like the pixies of Celtic mythology? But the name comes from Latin and Greek and has nothing whatsoever to do with elves. In full, the plant is *Pyxidanthera barbulata,* and the name was compounded by André Michaux, a French botanist in the New World. (See PHACELIA.) This small flower's formidable title, if

PYXIE

loosely translated, means "the barbed plant whose anthers bear seed capsules that open like a box."

Pyx is the Latin for box, from the Greek *pyxis,* and pyx is still used for the box or container in which communion wafers are kept. In this instance, pyx refers to the seed capsule that's shaped like a round box and has a lid that falls off to release the seeds. Anther comes from the Greek *anthos,* or flower, and is the enlarged part of the stamen that holds the pollen. Because of the plant's needle-like leaves, you have the Latin *barbulata,* or barbed. All in all, pyxie is a pretty and easily remembered nickname. Flowering moss is another, but far less specific or personal.

If we had been a few weeks earlier, we would have found two other flowers of spring we had enjoyed on previous visits to the barrens—the swamp pink, with its cloud of delicate lilac blooms, and the pyxie of the pine barrens, the matted mosslike flowering plant on which André Michaux, in 1803, bestowed the name *Pyxidanthera barbulata.* What hepatica and bloodroot are to the rich floor of the woodland, pyxie moss is to the barrens. It leads the parade of the spring flowers. One year on the thirty-first of March, when the barrens were still dun and wintry I came upon a dense mass of pyxie moss . . . across which a host of tiny, waxy-white flowers were scattered like snowflakes. . . . The acid, inhospitable soil of

169

the barrens, soil that repels most other vegetation, provides, paradoxically enough, the only environment in which Pyxidanthera can survive. Its entire range is limited to small areas on the Atlantic coast. Only in pine barrens between New Jersey and South Carolina—only here in all the world—does this flower of spring appear.
—EDWIN WAY TEALE, *North with the Spring*, 1956

RAGGED SAILOR. See KNAPWEED

RATTLESNAKE PLANTAIN — A native American orchid with a stalk of twining flowers that grows from a flat circle of checkered leaves. The Indians had complete faith in this plant as an infallible antidote against the bite of a rattler or any other venomous snake. In the late 1700's, a trader among the southern Indians wrote that each one carried a piece of the "best snake-root in his shot-pouch," and that he had never seen nor heard of any Indian dying from the bite of a snake.

The choice of the name plantain for this delicate ORCHID was evoked by its low-lying leaves, which, like the English and common PLANTAIN, derives from *planta*—Latin for the sole of the foot.

When an Indian perceives he is struck by a snake, he immediately chews some of the root, and having swallowed a sufficient quantity of it, he applies some to the wound, which he repeats as occasion requires, and in proportion to the poison the snake has infused into the wound. For a short space of time, there is a terrible conflict through all the body, by the jarring qualities of the burning poison, and the strong antidote; but the poison is soon repelled through the same channels it entered, and the patient is cured.
—JAMES ADAIR, *The History of the American Indians*, 1775

Country people use a decoction of the leaves for skin diseases, and the Indians are so convinced of its power as an antidote that they allow a snake to drive its fangs into them, then chew the leaves and apply them to the wound.—SAMUEL STEARNS, *American Herbal*, 1801

June 12, 1853. . . . The leaf of the rattlesnake plantain now surprises the walker amid the dry leaves on cool hill-sides in the woods; of very simple form, but richly veined with longitudinal and transverse white veins. It looks like art.—HENRY DAVID THOREAU, *Journals*

R H O D O D E N D R O N means "rose-tree" in Greek: *rhodon*, rose, and *dendron*, tree. It was an ancient name coined for flowering shrubs in the Mediterranean world, and when Linnaeus was searching for a descriptive title to give these new-discovered flowering shrubs from the New World, he reached back into the distant past and picked rhododendron.

As so often happened with American flora, rhododendrons were shipped to Europe to be fostered and oh-ed and ah-ed over, while Americans were still indifferent to the cultivation of native species. In the 1700's and 1800's, European gardens were ablaze with hybrid rhododendrons, not only created from American stock, but also from the first of the magnificent varieties discovered in the hinterlands of southeastern Asia. The rhododendron was brought to perfection in England, but it was not until the Centennial Exposition in Philadelphia, 1876, that Americans got a full view of the new varieties. A dazzling display was exhibited by an English nurseryman; the names alone were dazzling enough —the Countess of Cadogan, Princess of Wales, Sir Robert Peel, Princess Mary of Cambridge, Duchess of Bedford, Lady Olivia Guinness. Any number of patriotic flower lovers were pleased to point out that the blood of our native stock flowed in the veins of these noble British hybrids.

Meanwhile, in the back country, our wild rhododendrons were called deertongue and bigleaf, and the thickets of rhododendron that jungled the mountainsides were so dense, they were known as "hells" to the old-timers.

As soon as we had wearily dragged to the top of one hill, we began to rumble down the other side as rapidly as our four horses could trot; and no sooner arrived at the bottom than we began to crawl up again. . . . The latter part of the day, however, amply repaid us. At four o'clock we began to ascend the Alleghany mountains. . . . The whole of this mountain region, through ninety miles of which the road passes, is a garden. The almost incredible variety of plants, and the lavish profusion of their growth, produce an effect perfectly enchanting. . . . The magnificent rhododendron first caught our eyes; it fringes every cliff, nestles beneath every rock, and blooms around every tree. . . . All that is noblest in nature was joined to all that is sweetest.—Mrs. Frances Trollope, *Domestic Manners of the Americans*, 1832

June 4, 1853. The date of the introduction of the *Rhododendron maximum* into Concord is worth preserving. May, 1853. They were small plants one to four feet high, some with large flower buds, twenty-five cents apiece, and I noticed the next day one or more in every front yard on each side of the street, and the inhabitants out watering. Said to be the most splendid native flower in Massachusetts . . . I hear today that one in town has blossomed.—Henry David Thoreau, *Journals*

Tradition has it that Rhododendron hides the moonshiner and his still, and tradition is frequently right. Rhododendron may even play its part in the excessive isolation of mountain life; too high to see over, yet low enough to form an impenetrable twiggy thicket of crooked stems. . . . Nothing is easier than to get lost in the Rhodendron thickets, especially where the terrain is very steep. Commonly one used to see, in the country post offices of the southern mountains, notices of persons lost in the mountains.

If Rhododendron is a somber and even a menacing growth, at its most formidable, it is also one of the loveliest. . . At precisely that season when the shade grows dense and the breath of the valley is hot, when the thrush sings more and more briefly at dawn and after sunset, and all the other nine species of Rhododendron in the southern Appalachians have long since bloomed themselves out, the Big Rhododendron (*Rhododendron maximum*) at last opens its great, cool blossoms from the immense buds. . . . It would be difficult to discover a lovelier flower in the American flora. Yet in the forest, Big Rhododendron in flower is not gaudy or showy; it is far surpassed in eye-taking splendor by its relative the Catawba Rhododendron that in June clothes the highest peaks of the southern Appalachians in purple.—DONALD CULROSS PEATTIE, *A Natural History of Trees*, 1958

R O C K E T. See DAME'S ROCKET

R O S E—The word rose, with all its lovely connotations, has no known meaning. The rose is a rose. In English, French, German, Danish, and Norwegian it is *rose*. In Italian, Spanish, Portuguese, and Russian it is *rosa*. In Swedish it is *ros*, in Danish *roos*, and in Hungarian *rozsa*. In Greek it is *rhodon* and in Latin *rosa*, again names with no translation, but because of the colors of the flowers, both of these words came to mean red, rose, or pink. Roseola is a rose-colored rash. Rhodochrosite is a manganese carbonate, pink to red in color. Rhodolite is a red or pink variety of garnet. Rhodomine is a synthetic red or pink dye. From the shape of the flower we have the word rosette, and we have rose windows in architecture—round, stylized patterns of the flower, with stained glass in radiating traceries. Rosary beads originally represented the Virgin's crown of roses, or *rosarium*, as her garland was called in Medieval Latin.

PRAIRIE ROSE

Among our native roses is the Carolina rose, the swamp rose, the northeastern rose, the prairie rose, the redwood rose, the California rose, the smooth rose, and the Nootka rose that grows northwards from California to Alaska. Nootka was the name given the Indians of that region by Captain Cook. As the story goes, when Cook landed on the northwest coast, the Indians who gathered said something that sounded like "Nootka" and pointed to the bay. Cook wrote the name down on his chart. But experts in the local language say that the only word it could have been means "Go round," and that the Indians were presumably giving the captain directions.

The long-stemmed American beauty rose of hothouse fame, and the state flower of the District of Columbia, is not American at all, but a French hybrid introduced to the U.S.A. in 1875 as the *Mme. Ferdinand Jamin*. The Cherokee rose, state flower of Georgia, was an early Chinese import that now grows wild throughout the south—a climbing rose with solitary white flowers often three inches across. According to legend it was given its American name when a Cherokee maiden carried one of these roses to the tent of a wounded soldier whom she loved.

The "salt spray rose," or *Rosa rugosa* (the Latin for wrinkled, because of its wrinkled leaves) isn't a native either, though wild thickets of it grow along our shores. It was also introduced from the Orient and is one of the few roses able to survive exposure to salt water. *Rosa multiflora*, with its clusters of small blossoms, is a Japanese variety that has taken off cross country, new clumps of it multiplying as though by spontaneous combustion. The sweet-briar, or eglantine, is another alien run wild, brought from Europe by the French and the English. Eglantine comes from the Old French *aiglent,* in turn from the Latin *aquilentum,* or prickly, obviously in reference to its thorns.

In the Civil War, the Cherokee Rose was often planted as a memorial on the graves of fallen heroes by their surviving comrades. And today, the sight of the white flowers of this Rose wells up from the heart of many a veteran scenes of carnage and strife

and brings back memories of comrades laid to rest beneath its shade.
—ERNEST WILSON, *Aristocrats of the Garden*, 1926

July 18, 1853. I think the blossom of the sweetbriar, eglantine (now in prime), is more delicate and interesting that that of the common wild roses, though smaller and paler, and without their spicy fragrance. But its fragrance is in its leaves all summer, and the form of the bush is handsomer, curving over from a considerable height in wreaths sprinkled with numerous flowers. They open out flat soon after sunrise. Flowers whitish in the middle, then pinkish rose, inclining to purple toward the edges.—HENRY DAVID THOREAU, *Journals*

Crossing the Sierras. September, 1850—Fine morning, and we were up early. Had the fore feet of my pack-pony shod. . . . We rode along the N. side of the lake, till we reached a narrow valley, with a rapid creek. Fine tall grass, and vast quantities of rose-bushes line the margin of the stream. Their seed-pods are as delightful as conserve. We ate many. I called this, "Rose-bush Creek." We continued up the valley looking for a good and secure camp-ground.
—J. GOLDSBOUROUGH BRUFF, *Gold Rush*, 1849–1851

South Dakota, 1837. The Indians, the babies, the chickens and mice seem leagued to destroy the flowers, and they well nigh succeeded. Our garden enclosure extends around the back and both ends of our large mission house. Shading our family room are morning glories and a rose bush . . . a shoot from this wild rose is seven feet high, the growth of a single season, and is laden with buds! You may wonder why I bestow any of my precious time on flowers, but my mind needs some such cheering relaxation.—*Written by the wife of Reverend Stephen Riggs, to her mother in Massachusetts.*

S A G E B R U S H—Here is another borrowed name, like marsh rosemary and cowslip and laurel and arbutus. In this case, the name was chosen because of the sagelike smell of the leaves.

As for the true sage, an herb native to the northern shores of the Mediterranean, its name comes from the Old French, *suage,* which comes from the Latin *salvia,* "the healing plant," from *salvus,* healthy or safe.

Though their scent is similar, our sagebrush belongs to quite another genus—the ARTEMISIA. On the west coast, the local sagebrush (*Artemisia Californica*) was valued by the Indians and the Spanish settlers as a panacea for any number of internal ills, as well as for wounds and ulcers. What's more, a bed made up with a few branches from the plant would be free of fleas—a useful bit of Indian lore popular with miners in the gold rush days.

The most famous of our sagebrush is the variety that covers miles upon miles of the western alkaline plains, the *Artemisia tridentata,* so-named because of the three "teeth" at the apex of its leaves. It's the state flower of Nevada.

There are many Artemisias for the scented garden—best of all is *A. tridentata,* a treasure we owe to the United States. The scent of these leaves when crushed is more pleasing than that of southernwood, for it is even more aromatic and sweeter, and after rain it scents the air for yards round. It must be wonderful to see this plant in masses in its native habitats in North-West America.—ELEANOUR SINCLAIR RHODE, *The Scented Garden,* 1931

The principal growth, on plain and hill alike, was the interminable sagebrush, and often it was difficult, for miles at a time, to break a road through it, and sometimes a lightly laden wagon would be overturned. Its monotonous dull color and scraggy appearance gave a most dreary aspect to the landscape. But it was not wholly useless. Where large enough it made excellent fuel, and it was the home and shelter of the hare—generally known as the jackrabbit—and of the sage hen. Trees were almost a sure sign of water in that region. But the mirage was most deceptive, magnifying stunted sagebrush or dimunitive hillocks into trees and grove. Thus misled, we traveled all day without water, and at midnight found ourselves in a plain as level as a floor, incrusted with salt and as white as snow . . . In fact, we were going direct to Salt Lake and did not know it. —GEN. JOHN BIDWELL, *An Account of the First Emigrant Train to California,* 1839

176

Poetry!—just look round you,—alkali, rock, and sage;
Sage-brush, rock, and alkali; ain't it a pretty page!
—BRET HARTE, 1836–1902
Alkali Station

S T . J O H N S W O R T—In Teutonic mythology these
plants were dedicated to Baldur, the sun god, because their yellow flowers come into bloom around Mid-summer's Day, June
24, when the sun is in the sky longer than on any other day of
the year and the great sun god festivals were held. With the
Christian calendar, June 24 became St. John the Baptist's feast
day, and Baldur's yellow flowers were dedicated to St. John. From
then on, it was St. Johnswort—though still surrounded with ancient Teutonic superstitions and nicknamed "demon chaser."
When gathered on Mid-summer's Eve, it would ward off imps,
evil spirits, and the demons of melancholy. Hung in doorways and
windows, or carried in the pocket, it was a safeguard against
thunder and witches. But on the Isle of Wight, far from chasing
demons, St. Johnswort conjured them up. If you stepped on the
plant after dark, a phantom horse would rise from the roots, sweep
you up on its back, and gallop away with you through the whole
night long.
    There are several dozen native species throughout North
America, ranging from a dwarf St. Johnswort with flowers less
than a quarter of an inch across, to the great St. Johnswort
that reaches six feet in height and has magnificent yellow blossoms, several inches wide. The most prevalent of all is an alien
from Europe—the common St. Johnswort, a raggle-taggle, untidy
plant that grows throughout the country in fields, waste places,
and on roadsides. Many of the attractive varieties—American,
European, and Asian—are cultivated for the garden and listed in
nursery catalogues as *Hypericum,* the name given by the Greeks:
hyper, over, and *ereike,* heath. This evidently refers to the sandy
or loamy soil in which most St. Johnsworts will thrive. That is,
"it grows over the heath."

In ancient medicine, the juice of the St. Johnsworts was used as a vulnerary and the plants were known in England as "balm-of-the-warrior's-wound." The American Indians had discovered the same properties in our native species and made an oil from the sap to heal wounds, as well as using it for consumption.

> The leaves, floures, and seeds stamped, and put into a glasse with oyle Olive . . . doth make an oyle the colour of bloud, which is a most precious rememdy for deepe wounds, and those that are through the body, for sinews that are prickt, or any wound made with a venomed weapon. I am accustomed to make a compound oyle hereof; the making of which ye shall receive at my hands; for I dare undertake to cure any such wound as absolutely in each respect, if not sooner and better, as any man whatsoever.—JOHN GERARD, *Herbal*, 1597

> *June, 1776. Flint River, Georgia.* At evening we came to camp near the banks of a large and deep creek, a branch of the Flint. The high land excellent, affording grand forests, and the low ground vast timber and Canes of great height and thickness. I observed growing on the steep dry banks of this creek, a species of shrub Hypericum, of extraordinary show and beauty. It grows erect, three or four feet high, forming a globular top, representing a perfect little tree; the leaves are large, oblong, firm of texture, smooth and shining; the flowers are very large, their petals broad and conspicuous, which, with their tufts of golden filaments, give the little bushes a very splendid appearance.—WILLIAM BARTRAM, *Travels*, 1773–1777

SARSAPARILLA—We have several wild, so-called sarsaparillas native to America, but the true sarsaparilla is a Caribbean and Mexican plant named by the Spaniards. They coined *zarzaparilla* from *zarza*, meaning a bramble or bush, and *parilla*, which is the diminutive of *parra*, or vine. So it means "the little vine bush," a fine descriptive name for this climbing plant.

Our native "sarsaparillas" are quite different—a leafy plant with white flower clusters typical of the GINSENG family to which they belong. But their roots have the same taste as the true sarsaparillas, and thus the name was picked up in popular usage.

When the true sarsaparillas were introduced to Europe by the Spaniards, they were first used in medicine as a specific for rheumatism, syphilis, and poisons, "whether they be drunk before or after." Meantime, the American Indians were using our wild sarsaparillas in their medicines and John Winthrop prescribed it for palsy. The true sarsaparillas were found to be delicious additives to unfermented beers brewed from aromatic rootstocks, much like the ones we drink today—root beer, birch beer, and sarsaparilla. Our wild sarsaparillas were found to be a good replacement, though not as tasty as the real article, but they would do in a pinch. The roots of our native brand, chopped fine, can also be made into a tea.

Wild Sarsaparilla. Montagnais and Penobscot women cut up the roots, tied the pieces on a string, and kept them in their lodges until needed. Montagnais Indians fermented the berries in water for a wine used as a tonic. The Penobscots dried the roots, crushed them to powder, and steeped the substance together with roots of sweet flag for a cough medicine. The Catawbas boiled the root for a tea which was sweetened with sugar and taken as a tonic and health beverage. Flambeau Ojibwas pounded the root for a poultice for boils and carbuncles. Pillager Ojibwa women used it for "purification" in pregnancy. The Potawatomis used the pounded root for a poultice on swellings and infections.—VIRGIL J. VOGEL, *American Indian Medicine,* 1970

The wild sarsaparilla, which must not be mistaken for the true sarsaparilla of soda-water fame, is nevertheless often used as a substitute for the official article. Its slender roots, which run horizontally three or four feet in every direction away from the stem, are as aromatic as the mucilaginous twigs of the sassafras tree. But every country boy knows all about sassafras and sarsaparilla; any plant which appeals to his sense of taste or his propensity to chew is a component part of the well-digested knowledge he never learned at school. The rather pretty balls of fine greenish-white flowers of unique appearance, which bloom early in summer, will easily enable one to identify the plant.—SCHUYLER MATHEWS, *Familiar Flowers of Field and Garden,* 1895

SAXIFRAGE is the rock-breaker, from the Latin *saxum,* a stone, and *frangere,* to break. There are some three hundred and seventy saxifrages all told, with sixty-five species native to North America, and every variety has the same fondness for growing in the crevices of rocks, where little else can get a toe-hold. Therefore, its name, because it seemed to crack open the rocks among which it grew. And as a "rock-breaker," saxifrages were used in ancient medicine to break down kidney stones. Among the first of the spring flowers, an old nickname is none-so-pretty.

April 10, 1853. The saxifrage is beginning to be abundant, elevating its flowers somewhat, pure trustful white amid its pretty notched and reddish cup of leaves . . . a response from earth to the increased light of the year.—HENRY DAVID THOREAU, *Journals*

*June 10, 1869—*We get water for the camp from a rock basin at the foot of a picturesque cascading reach of the river. . . . The giant saxifrage is growing on some of the knob rock islets, firmly anchored and displaying their broad round umbrella-like leaves in showy groups. The flowers of this species are purple, and form tall glandular racemes that are in bloom before the appearance of the leaves. The fleshy root-stocks grip the rock in cracks and hollows, and thus enable the plant to hold on against occasional floods—a marked species employed by Nature to make yet more beautiful the most interesting portions of these cool clear streams. Near camp the trees arch over from bank to bank, making a leafy tunnel full of soft subdued light, through which the young river sings and shines like a happy living creature.—JOHN MUIR, *My First Summer in the Sierra,* 1911

None of the Saxifrages seem to have excited poetic fire, nor have they entered in any way into the arts. . . . Before it flowers it forms one of the most beautiful rosettes imaginable. For the central ornament in a piece of carving, it would furnish an admirable pattern. With the warm weather, the green of the leaves becomes prettily tinted with rose, and at this stage the plant is in nice condition for the artist, to whom these departing shades in the sunset of plant-life are always welcome.—THOMAS MEEHAN, *The Native Ferns and Flowers of the United States,* 1880

I have always been a fervent advocate of birth-control, but since I have been the owner of a rock garden my fervour has increased a hundred-fold. The prolificacy of the common saxifrage is positively embarrassing. . . . Forgive me. I ought not to have spoken disparagingly of the generosity of these delightful plants. It is really rather caddish to sneer at a saxifrage which climbs, so bravely, from rock to rock, bearing its sweet standards aloft, carrying to the barren lands a rosy glow of hope. These are valiant flowers, and gay, and sturdy. For us, the rocks are not so easily scaled, nor the darkness so sweetly illuminated.—BEVERLEY NICHOLS, *Down the Garden Path*, 1932

S C U P P E R N O N G—The American grape said to have been first discovered on Roanoke Island by Sir Walter Raleigh's doomed colonists. The name came from the Scuppernong River, which was called the *Askuponong* by the Virginian Indians—"at the place of the magnolia." *Askupo* was the word for magnolia.

These are a southern species of grape, too tender for the northern climates. They grow in small bunches, either with light green or dark red fruit that is juicy and sweet with a rather musky scent and flavor.

To Justice William Johnson, of the Supreme Court. . . . The pamphlet you were so kind as to send me manifests a zeal, which cannot be too much praised, for the interests of agriculture, the employment of our first parents in Eden, the happiest we can follow. . . . I am not without hope that thro' your efforts and example, we shall yet see it a country abounding in wine and oil. North Carolina has the merit of taking the lead in the former culture, of giving the first specimen of an exquisite wine, produced in quantity. . . . Her Scuppernon wine, made on the Southside of the Sound, would be distinguished on the best tables of Europe, for its fine aroma, and chrystalline transparence . . . —THOMAS JEFFERSON, Monticello, May 10, 1817

The Scuppernong grape is not a Florida native, but cuttings from old Carolina and Georgia vines have been brought in with many a covered wagon and on many an ox-cart. The vine thrives here in

SCUPPERNONG GRAPE

the dry sandy soil, and on many abandoned clearings, where even the brick chimneys have fallen into dust, a huge Scuppernong will stand . . . an echo of some dead and gone family struggle for existence . . . the white Scuppernong, in the hands of loving and expert care, makes a vintage white wine that can stand with the best Sauterne.

When Selma and I were taking the census, we came on an old man far off in the piney-woods who gave us cups of white Scuppernong wine so dry, so fine, that I could not believe my palate.—MARJORIE KINNAN RAWLINGS, *Cross Creek*, 1942

SEGO LILY. See MARIPOSA

SHINLEAF. See PYROLA

SKUNK CABBAGE. See under ARUM

SNAKE-MOUTH. See POGONIA

SNAPWEED. See TOUCH-ME-NOT

SNOW-ON-THE-MOUNTAIN. See SPURGE

SOAPWORT, or Bouncing Bet. See under WORT

SOLOMON'S SEAL, a tall curving spray of leaves with small greenish-yellow bell-like flowers hanging in pairs along the stalk; native to America, Europe, and across the Asian continent to Japan.

This is an ancient name, the English translation of the original Latin *Sigillum Salomonis,* and has been much disputed. According to one theory, it came from the appearance of the tuberous roots that carry round scars left by flower stalks from previous years. These round scars were compared to Solomon's seal, or signet. Incidentally, you can tell the age of these plants by the number of stem scars on the roots, one for each year, just as you can count the rings of yearly growth in the cross section of a tree trunk.

According to another theory, the name comes from the plant's age-old use as a balm to seal, or close, fresh wounds. John Gerard has this to say on the question, in 1597: "Dioscorides writeth, That the roots are excellent good for to seale up greene wounds; whereupon it was called Sigillum Salomonis, of the singular vertue that it hath in sealing up or healing up wounds, broken bones, and such like. Some thought it tooke the name Sigillum of the markes upon the roots: but the first reason seemes to me more probable." Gerard further added that the root "taketh away in one night, or two at the most, any bruise, blacke or blew spots gotten by falls or womens wilfulnesses in stumbling upon their hasty husbands fists, or such like."

But in all of this, the question of Solomon's name being attached to the plant has never been resolved. The Greeks, of course, had given it their own earlier name—*polygonatum,* or "many knees," because of the many root joints, and this is still the botanic designation. The title of Solomon's seal was introduced in the early Christian era, and I have my own theory on this choice, for what it may be worth. The plant has six-petaled flowers—six points to each blossom, like the six points of the Star of David, which in early days was always known as Solomon's seal. Perhaps

183

the original meaning was forgotten, and the seals seen on the roots and its use as a sealer of wounds gave rise to the later interpretations.

The several varieties of FALSE SOLOMON'S SEAL are native to North America only—sprays of leaves with a tuft of starry, white flowers and often with an irregular stalk, that prompted the nickname "zig-zag." Both the false and true Solomon's seals belong to the lily family and because their leaves and stalks are similar, the old European name was passed on.

An overgrown path led to the darkest part of the woods, to the wild strawberry blossoms, the tall, slender stalks of Solomon's seal and the ferns, with their freshly opened fronds.—COLETTE, *Duo*, 1935

The false Solomon's seal is in my estimation even more beautiful than the true. Its spike of fine white flowers is like the *Spirea Japonica*; besides, its wary, bright green leaf with the parallel veining is particularly graceful. Most wild flowers, like the true Solomon's seal, have rather insignificant blossoms; but there is nothing meager about the bloom of this little plant. It deserves cultivation, and, in truth, if it is transplanted to a position in the garden similar to its natural environment, it will flourish most satisfactorily. It is a shame that any aspersion of falsity should attach to it; why should not a plant so deserving have its own good name? We might as well call a Frenchman a false Englishman! . . . It seems as though our nation was lacking in both originality and imagination!—F. SCHUYLER MATTHEWS, *Familiar Flowers of Field and Garden*, 1895

SORREL is "sour"—from the Old High German *sur*; sour grass is one nickname. *Oxalis*, the botanic name, also means sour, from the Greek *oxys*. And the leaves are indeed sour, with a distinct acid flavor. This is an international tribe, all with cloverlike leaves. In Ireland, it is the shamrock, which comes from the Gaelic *seamrag*, a diminutive for clover. In America, we have yellow wood sorrels, violet, and white or pink with purple veining —the same color combination as the shamrock and the common sorrel of Europe. "Alleluia" is a nickname in English as well as

COMMON WOOD SORREL (OXALIS)

in various European languages, because the flowers bloom in the Easter season, "at which time *Alleluya* was wont to be sung in churches."

Because of the heart-shaped leaves, early herbalists took this as a heaven-ordained sign that wood sorrel was a cure for all cardiac diseases. The plants were also valued as antiscorbutics. In Lapland, for example, sorrel was boiled with milk into a coagulated mass that was stored in underground casks as winter food when there were no fresh greens to be had.

However, wood sorrel or *oxalis,* is not considered the true sorrel by botanists. True sorrel has halberd-shaped leaves and is classified as *Rumex,* the original Latin name with no known meaning other than "sorrel." The *Rumex* were used as culinary herbs by the Egyptians, Greeks, and Romans, and Horace recommended it "with a cup of Coan wine" for queasy stomachs, the Roman propensity for feasting and over-eating being what it was. Among the *Rumex* family, several made their way to America—such "weeds" as those that we call sheep sorrel, garden sorrel, broad or bitter dock, and curled dock. Sheep sorrel has a tasty, lemonish flavor and is delicious in salads and sauces. The young leaves of curled dock can be eaten like spinach and are loaded with protein and Vitamin A.

Our native *Rumex,* as well as the European species that spread like wildfire, were used in Indian medicines—for jaundice, boils, sore throats, blood purifiers, and poison antidotes.

June 12, 1852. Some fields are almost wholly covered with sheep's sorrel, now turned red. . . . It helps thus agreeably to paint the earth, contrasting even at a distance with the greener fields, blue sky, and dark or downy clouds. It is red, marbled, mottled, or waved with greenish, like waving grain, three or four acres of it. To the farmer or grazier it is a troublesome weed, but to the landscape viewer, an agreeable red tinge laid on by the painter. I feel well into summer when I see this red tinge. It appears to be avoided by the cows.—Henry David Thoreau, *Journals*

Great Yellow Wood-Sorrel. In the hollows of bare and often unsympathetic looking places along the river's banks, this great one of the *Oxalis* tribe forms often thick and rounded clumps of its clover-like leaves, and throws out its cheer-countenanced little blossoms. They always seem fresh and wide awake, perhaps because in accordance with the old maxim they so early in the evening fold their leaflets together and then unfold them with the first gleam of morning sun.—Alice Lounsberry, *Guide to Wildflowers,* 1899

S P I C E B U S H. See Benjamin Bush

S P U R G E—A word with a decidedly quaint, Old World ring to it. But the meaning is purely cautionary. Spurge comes from the Latin *purgare,* to purge, and the milky juice of all members of this vast family is a dangerous cathartic and emetic. Devil's milk and wolf's milk were old nicknames. Also, widow's wail, because it could be fatal. A few drops, but only a few, were recommended for eating away warts, callouses, carbuncles, leprosies, and similar afflictions.

Another unique feature of this family is their false flowers. What looks like petals are really brightly colored bracts, and the flowers themselves are tiny—insignificant, in fact, without a magnifying glass. The poinsettia, native to Mexico, is a spurge; those red and white petals are leaves. Their name in Spanish is *flor de nochebuena,* "the flower of Christmas Eve," but when they were introduced to America by Joel Poinsett, our minister to

Mexico in the 1820's and later Van Buren's secretary of war, they were given his name. Poinsett, famed in his day for the creme-de-la-creme parties at his Charleston estate (only the beautiful and the witty were invited), was also renowned as a first-rate horticulturist, and he raised all manner of rare plants in his Charleston garden, among them the poinsettia that bore his name.

The cypress spurge, so called because of its cypress-like leaves, was brought to America principally as a grave flower—all in the tradition of the cypress trees from which funeral garlands had been made since antiquity, because of the long life of the leaves after they were cut. (*Cypress* is a Greek word with no known meaning.) Indeed, the cypress spurge I have seen over the years was usually in and around old cemeteries, and it was once known in New England as graveyard ground pine. A more cheerful nickname was love-in-a-huddle, because of its closely bunched blossoms. These flower clusters were also the reason for another old name, "seven sisters," which was borrowed from the Pleiades, a cluster of many stars.

Our flowering spurge is a native and looks like a small daisy, but unlike daisies the white rays are leaves and the yellow heart is the flower. It was recognized by the Indians as a powerful cathartic and was used, as were other local spurges, in carefully considered doses.

Snow-on-the-mountain, a spurge native to the drier parts of our country from the Missouri to the Rockies was first listed by the Lewis and Clark expedition (1804–1806). Now a garden pet, snow-on-the-mountain was given its descriptive name by early settlers. The green leaves with their snowy white margins made the plant "particularly attractive to the traveller over these far western railroads," Thomas Meehan wrote in 1880. "It is in its best dress where the soil has been disturbed. It is more than probable that at no very distant date it will be found up to the shores of the Atlantic ocean." Meehan's prophecy came true. Not only did snow-on-the-mountain move eastward along the new railroad lines, but it was also transplanted to eastern gardens—and escaped.

The list of spurges, native and alien, could go on and on. Suffice to say that they belong to the worldwide tribe of *Euphorbias*. Pliny tells us that the first spurges were found on Mount Atlas by King Juba of Mauritanis, who gave them their name in honor of his favorite physician, Euphorbus.

On roaming the shelves of a second-hand bookshop. I often take down one or another of the brown-paged early editions of Asa Gray's *Manual of Botany*, that begins in the old style with the buttercups and ends with the ferns or mosses. I finger the leaves affectionately, not so much for good Asa's sake, as because I respect the one-time owners, whose names I like to read in the covers of these books—the sterling Felicias and forthright Amasas of a bygone generation. I like to shake the faded wisp of a jewelweed or a birdfoot violet out of the leaves, where it was pressed some summer long ago. And I always turn over toward the back to the Euphorbia family, fairly confident that there I shall find a sprig of flowering spurge, the amateur's stumbling block. And there I find it, where it was left, a landmark, a triumphant monument to persistence. —Donald Culross Peattie, *An Almanac for Moderns*, 1935

This cypress spurge, too, is deserving of more than passing mention. Every walker should know it and pay his tribute of appreciation to its autumn beauty, for these is no such subtle play and blending of color to be found elsewhere in a single plant in the whole array of October tints. A bed of it gives the effect of being lit up from some illuminated window—a strange melting quality of color. It is like a small sunset cloud floating on the grass. Note the color in this single spray: from the richest of pure greens . . . to olive to purple, with blue reflections, to purple maroon, deep crimson, scarlet, pink, orange, and gradually culminating in the purest yellow—the modulation so soft and subtle that scarcely any two leaves of these hundreds are of precisely the same shade. This species of spurge is not common, being found only where its association with some old cellar or garden site betrays its escape from earlier cultivation.—William Hamilton Gibson, *Happy Hunting Grounds*, 1886

Mr. Vick:—I thought I would tell you what an adventure I had with the Euphorbia or Snow-on-the-mountain. A few evenings ago I went to make bouquets for my friends, and I kept plucking now and then a sprig of Euphorbia to mingle in with the scarlet and pink Geraniums; they contrast so beautifully with its snowy-white and green leaves. As you are aware, it contains a milky, acrid juice. The evening being very warm I would occasionally wipe my face with my hands, not knowing the danger. Soon after my face and eyes commenced smarting and burning, and next morning my face and one eye was badly swollen, and also attended with nauseau and dizziness.

My husband thought best to dig it up and cast it away, but I still plead for its life, though I do believe if a child should unknowingly eat a small quantity, it would prove a deadly poison. While out on my lawn this evening, I could not help looking at it with a little contempt, that, after all my tender, watchful care, it would treat me so unkindly; and it looks so pure and innocent.

Now, Mr. Vick, I have one request to make. Wont you give us one of your pictures in your magazine before the close of the year, instead of a floral chromo?—Mrs. A.H., Bantam, O.

The Euphorbias all have an acid juice that is more or less irritating to the skin. Some persons may handle the milky juice with impunity; to others it is quite irritating. . . . We receive many such suggestions about a portrait, but as we are getting better looking every day, a little delay will be of mutual advantage.—*Vick's Magazine*, October, 1879

STAGGER-BUSH. See under ANDROMEDA

STAGGER-GRASS. See ATAMASCO LILY

STAR-THISTLE. See KNAPWEED

STINKING BENJAMIN. See TRILLIUM

STRAWBERRY—In Anglo-Saxon the word was *streawberige*. *Streaw* meant stew and was given because a strawberry vine spreads by strewing its runners—by spreading them

AMERICAN WILD
STRAWBERRY

out, in other words. And *streaw* is also the root word for straw, because grass was strewn, or spread out, to dry into hay and straw. *Berige*, or berry, is similar to words in Danish, Swedish, German, Icelandic, and others of the northern European languages, all meaning the same: an edible fruit, a berry. The Romans called strawberries *fragaria*, because of their fragrance, and this remains the scientific name.

Roger Williams, the founder of Rhode Island, wrote that the Indians bruised wild strawberries in a mortar, mixed them with meal, and made strawberry-bread. "This berry," he declared, "is the wonder of all the fruits growing naturally in these parts. . . . Where the natives have planted, I have many times seen as many as would fill a good ship, within a few miles' compass."

It was Izaac Walton who recorded and immortalized the famous quote: "Doubtless God could have made a better berry, but doubtless God never did." Man, however, got busy and tried to make a better berry with the first serious cultivation of strawberries, in Europe, in the fifteenth century. In the late 1600's one of the wild strawberries of America, *Fragaria virginiana*, and another from Chile, *Fragaria chileonsis*, were crossed in England to create new and delicious hybrids, known in those days as "English strawberries." (But the flavor of wild strawberries, eaten from the vine, can never be matched.)

Our wild plants, with their leaves of three and five-petaled flowers, are often confused with CINQUEFOIL.

June, 1776. On the Little Tennessee River. . . . We enjoyed a

190

most enchanting view—a vast expanse of green meadows and strawberry fields, a meandering river gliding through, turfy knolls em-
bellished with parterres of flowers and fruitful strawberry beds,
flocks of turkeys strolling about them, herds of deer prancing in the
meads or bounding over the hills, companies of young, innocent
Cherokee virgins, some busy gathering the rich, fragrant fruit.
Others, having already filled their baskets, lay reclined under the
shade of floriferous and fragrant native bowers . . . disclosing their
beauties to the fluttering breeze and bathing their limbs in the cool,
fleeting streams; whilst other parties, more gay and libertine, were
yet collecting strawberries, or wantonly chasing their companions, tantalizing them, staining their lips and cheeks with the
rich fruit. . . .

Now, although we meant no other than an innocent frolic with
this gay assembly of hamadryads, we shall leave it to the person of
feeling and sensibility to form an idea to what lengths our passions
might have hurried us, thus warmed and excited, had it not been
for the vigilance and care of some matrons who lay in ambush and
gave the alarm, time enough for the nymphs to rally and assemble
together . . . peeping through the bushes. Observing our ap-
proaches, they confidently discovered themselves and decently
advanced to meet us, half unveiling their blooming faces, incar-
nated with the modest maiden blush, and cheerfully presented their
little baskets, merrily telling us their fruit was ripe and sound.

We accepted a basket, sat down and regaled ourselves on the
delicious fruit, encircled by the whole assembly of the innocent,
jocose sylvan nymphs . . . under the conduct of the elder matrons.
—William Bartram, *Travels*, 1773–1777

Beyond the road where the snakes sunned themselves was a
dense young thicket, and through it a dim-lighted path led a quarter of a mile; then out of the dimness one emerged abruptly upon
a level great prairie which was covered with wild strawberry plants,
vividly starred with prairie pinks, and walled in on all sides by
forests. The strawberries were fragrant and fine, and in the season
we were generally there in the crisp freshness of the early morning,
while the dew beads still sparkled upon the grass and the woods
were ringing with the first songs of the birds.—Mark Twain,
1835–1910, *Autobiography*

SWAMP-CANDLE. See under LOOSESTRIFE

SWEET-WILLIAM, WILD. See under PHLOX

TANSY—Round, yellow flowers and leaves "infinitely jagged and nicked and curled withall, like unto a plume of feathers," with a pungent odor that smells to *me* like pine needles and wintergreen and perhaps a dash of sweet fern. The name comes from the Old French *tanesie*, which came from the Greek *athanasia*, or immortality; *a*, not, and *thanatos*, death. Presumably this name was prompted because of the tansy's long-lived scent and medical usefulness. The tea brewed from it in the old days has been described as "perfectly vile-tasting" and worse than the ailments it was intended to cure—such as rheumatism and "bringing out" the measles; tansy tea's age-old reputation as an abortive persists to this day.

Around the fifteenth century, the custom arose of eating paschal cakes made with tansy juice in rememberance of the bitter herbs eaten by the Jews at Passover. Eventually the bitter tansy cakes were superseded by tansy puddings made with sugar, rosewater, eggs, cream, etcetera. In 1666, Samuel Pepys served a "pretty dinner" to guests, consisting of "a brace of stewed carps, six roasted chickens, and a jowl of salmon hot, for the first course; a tansy, two neat's tongues, and a cheese, the second."

With all these traditions behind it, tansy was one of the treasured plants brought to the New World, and John Josselyn, who visited New England in 1638 and 1663, listed "tansie" as a garden herb flourishing in the colonies. It inevitably escaped and is now one of our wildflowers. Another common name is bitter buttons, because of its taste and the shape of the flowers.

On July 1, 1846, an old grave was opened in the ancient "God's

Acre" near the halls of Harvard University in Cambridge, Massachusetts. This grave was a brick vault covered with irregularly shaped flagstones about three inches thick. . . . When the coffin was opened, the skeleton was found entirely surrounded with common Tansy, in seed, a portion of which had been pulled up by the roots. . . . The tansy found in this coffin, placed there more than two centuries ago, still retained its shape and scent.

This use of Tansy at funerals lingered long in country neighborhoods in New England, in some vicinities till fifty years ago. To many older persons the Tansy is therefore so associated with grewsome sights and sad scenes. One elderly friend write me: "I never see the leaves of Tansy without recalling also the pale dead faces I have so often seen encircled by the dank, ugly leaves. Often as a child have I been sent to gather all the Tansy I could find, to be carried by my mother to the house of mourning; and I gathered it, loathing to touch it, but not daring to refuse, and I loath it still. —ALICE MORSE EARLE, *Old Time Gardens*, 1901

Every year I see the tansy grow a little commoner hereabout. It is still a rare plant, but not in the sense that it is sought after or prized when it is found. A waif from the Old World, an outcast from gardens, with its ferny dark foliage and golden button heads, it can still claim kinship to a royal line of flowers, for it is but a chrysanthemum without the rays. The aroma of its leaves is closest to that of French marigolds, yet a little similar, also, to the smell of yarrow, of camomile or marguerite. A bitter oil pervades the plant, from which our grandmothers were wont to brew a nasty and I think quite harmful medicament, and it is this that on the quiet dusty airs of autumn afternoons distills that odor that will remind me, wherever I breathe it, of New England walls, of autumn days at college when new friends were made, new thoughts encountered . . . —DONALD CULROSS PEATTIE, *An Almanac for Moderns*, 1935

T A R E. See VETCH

T H O R N - A P P L E. See JIMSONWEED

TICKSEED. See Coreopsis

TOADFLAX blooms at the end of summer, spruce and spring-like with its daffodil colors, small blossoms, and diminutive height. Compared to the other wildflowers of early Autumn—goldenrod, boneset, joe-pye weed—toadflax seems delicate. But delicate it is not. This is a pasture flower, a waste place flower, a roughneck flower that will grow anywhere.

The name toadflax puzzled me for years, but the reason for it is ridiculously obvious. As John Gerard explained in his 1597 *Herbal*: "Tode-flax hath small, slender, stalks; from which do grow many long narrow leaves like flax. The floures be yellow, having a mouth unto a frogs mouth." If you pinch the flower at the hinge of its jaw, the frog mouth opens—just like the dragon mouth of its southern European relative, the snapdragon.

Butter-and-eggs is the American nickname for toadflax, because of its colors. Another nickname, also of American origin, is ranstead or ramstead. According to Dr. John Darlington (1782–1836), who was a bank president in West Chester, Pennsylvania, and a dedicated botanist, the toadflax was introduced to America by a Welshman named Ranstead. Mr. Ranstead settled near Philadelphia, where so many of the colonial Welsh were found-

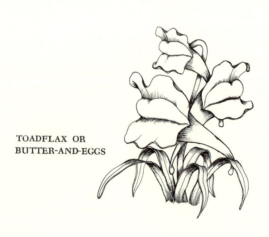

TOADFLAX OR
BUTTER-AND-EGGS

ing their Welsh communities—Bryn Mawr, Bryn Athyn, Bala-Cynwyd. Ranstead brought along toadflax, a common pasture flower in the British Isles, and planted it in the garden of his new home. From there, it supposedly took off on its non-stop conquest of North America. Whether Mr. Ranstead was the only one to bring toadflax to the New World we do not know, but it seems quite likely that others would import the plant for herb gardens since it had a good medical reputation in Europe—for treating yellow jaundice, piles, and conjunctivitis; boiled in milk it made an excellent fly poison. By 1785, the Reverend Manassah Cutler of Boston described toadflax as "a common, handsome, tedious weed." And when Dr. Darlington wrote about the flora of Chester County, Pennsylvania, early in the 1800's, he described toadflax as "showy, but very obnoxious."

The scent of toadflax has been described as a cheesey odor, like an un-aired dairy, and it has also been described as a faint, sweet fragrance. To me, it has an herbal sort of smell, almost medicinal.

The blue toadflax, which grows near the sea on either coast, is native to America. Again, opinions differ. I have seen it dismissed as small and insignificant, its flowers always in the dust and sand. On the other hand it has been poeticized for its charm and color.

The delicate blue flowers of the toad-flax are not uncommon in spring, and the plants are usually found in sandy soil. The little blossoms are very ethereal and have a sweet perfume. I once saw a deep blue band upon a mesa near San Diego, which vied in richness with the ultra marine of the sea just beyond. It stretched for some distance, and at last curved around and crossed the road over which I was passing, when it proved to be made up of millions of these delicate flowers.—MARY ELIZABETH PARSONS, *Wild Flowers of California*, 1900

Thirty years ago, in a locality I knew well in central Massachusetts, yellow Toad-flax, or Butter-and eggs, was far from common. I even remember the first time I saw it and was told its quaint names. It travels above ground and below ground, and in some soils will rout out the grass. It knows how to allure the bumblebees, however, and has honey in its heart. . . . The greatest beauty of this flower is in the autumn, when it springs up densely in shaven fields. I have seen, even in the last week in October, fields entirely filled with its exquisite sulphur-yellow tint, a yellow that is luminous at night . . . —ALICE MORSE EARLE, *Old Time Gardens*, 1901

TOUCH-ME-NOT—The name explains itself if you have seen the ripe pods that burst at the slightest touch, or even at a breath, and can fire their seeds to a distance of three or four feet. Impatience and snapweed are other nicknames, because of the haste with which they explode. Jewelweed and lady's eardrops are also commonly heard and again are self-explanatory when you see the blossoms. Among the Indians, the openmouthed shape of the flowers inspired the name "crowing cock," and they used the juice as a soothing astringent for poison ivy, nettle rash, and excema. Because of this soothing property, these plants are sometimes known as wild balsam, the name taken from a related garden variety; balsam once upon a time was an alternate word for balm, a word of Semitic origin, such as the Hebrew *basam* that meant a healing or aromatic ointment. (And that brings us right along to embalm and the ancient use of balms or aromatic oils to preserve the bodies of the dead.)

Touch-me-not, or *noli-me-tangere* as it is known in Latin, is sometimes called silverleaf, because the leaves, when wet, have a silvery iridescent sheen. And, as you will see in reading the quotation from Edwin Way Teale, the English invented yet one more nickname when these American flowers were introduced to the British Isles.

Towards the month of September there is a yellow flower which grows in great luxuriance along the sides of creeks and rivers, and in low moist situations; it grows to the height of two or three feet, and the flower which is about the size of a thimble, hangs in the shape of a cap of liberty above a luxuriant growth of green leaves. It is the *Balsamina noli me tangere* of botanists, and is the greatest favorite with the Humming Bird of all our other flowers. In some places where these plants abound you may see at one time ten or

TOUCH-ME-NOT

twelve Humming Birds darting about, and fighting with and pursuing each other. . . . When two males meet at the same bush, or flower, a battle instantly takes place; and the combatants ascend in the air, chirping, darting and circling round each other, till the eye is no longer able to follow them. The conqueror, however, generally returns to the place to reap the fruits of his victory. —ALEXANDER WILSON, 1766–1813, *American Ornithology*

The "touch-me-not," with its translucent, juicy stem, and its queer little golden flowers with spotted throats—the "jewel-weed" we used to call it. This is the dewy night's rarest treasure. It is indeed a jewel. Upon the approach of twilight each leaf droops as if wilted, and from the notches along its edge the crystal beads begin to grow, until its border is hung full with its gems. It is Aladdin's lantern that you set among a bed of these succulent green plants, for the spectacle is like dream land.—WILLIAM HAMILTON GIBSON, *Sharp Eyes*, 1892

Welcome visitors from across the sea are now part of the ancient forest. One is the jewelweed, or touch-me-not of eastern North America, called the orange balsam in Britain. Famous for its ripe fruits which explode and hurl out seeds when touched or brushed against, it bears pendant slipperlike orange-yellow flowers mottled with reddish brown. With that gift for bestowing picturesque flower names that has so often been demonstrated in the past, the

197

English call these alien blossoms "swing-boats."—Edwin Way
Teale, *Springtime in Britain*, 1970

T R I L L I U M is a word concocted by Linnaeus from *tri*,
the Latin for three, because everything about these plants is as-
sembled in sets of three—a whorl of three leaves, three sepals,
three petals, six stamens, three-cell ovaries, and three ribs on each
berry. The showiest trilliums are North American, with a few
lesser varieties native to Japan and the Himalayas.

The red trillium is the most common and goes by various nicknames: stinking benjamin, because of its scent; wake robin, because it blooms in early spring; and birthroot, because it was used
by the Indians and early settlers to ease childbirth. Though one
of the handsomest of the spring flowers, my turn of the century
wildflower books are scathing on the subject of red trillium: "It
repels us by its unpleasant odour. Its common name, while pretty,
does not wake the robins, because they have been chirping and
hopping about on lawns long before the flower came into bloom.
So altogether we are inclined to believe that the plant has too
great an idea of its own importance." And, "An unattractive, car-
rion-scented flower resembling in color and odor a raw beefsteak
of uncertain age."

However, the white trilliums and the painted trilliums (white
with red hearts) were universally admired and were among the
first American plants cultivated in English gardens. Toadshade
is another variety, named for the brown markings on its leaves,
with green, brown-purple, or yellow flowers.

We begin to look for the Californian Trillium early in the spring.
Little companies of the plants may be seen upon low flats under
the trees, where the soil is rich. The large leaves are often like pieces
of decorated china that have been several times through the kiln.
They have various superimposed blotchings, the latest of which are
dark, sharp, cuneiform characters, mysterious hieroglyphs of
Nature, which might reveal wondrous secrets, could we but deci-
pher them. The blossoms are exceedingly variable in color, ranging

from pure white to lilac, deep wine, and even black-purple . . .
—MARY ELIZABETH PARSONS, *Wild Flowers of California*, 1900

A trail, not a patch, not a clump, but a *trail* of giant white trillium wandered down the slope toward the stream. Enormous green triumvirate of leaves. Beautiful, the white curved petals on long stems. Three white wax petals, three green under the leaves— coiled and sailing as the coifs of Belgian nuns.—JOSEPHINE W. JOHNSON, *The Inland Island*, 1969

Pearson's Falls, near Tryon, North Carolina. Like the leaves of a partly opened book, the walls of the narrow glen rose steeply on either side. They were tilted flower fields, starred from top to bottom with the great waxy pink and white blooms of immense trilliums. Changing color as they grow older, some range from snowy white through pink to deep purple-pink before their petals wither. Our first and most lasting impression of the ravine was this trillium tapestry that ascended on either hand.—EDWIN WAY TEALE, *North with the Spring*, 1965

T R O U T   L I L Y—We have a white, a pink, and any number of yellow-to-orange varieties of these early woodland lilies, and most of them have speckled leaves—like the speckled markings of a trout. Trout lily, however, is a fairly recent American nickname; so is fawn lily, given because the spots on the leaves can also be compared to the spotting on a fawn. This last originally referred to a California species, but is coming into common use as a general name, as John Burroughs first suggested almost ninety years ago, though most wildflower guides have not picked up on it yet. Burroughs not only remarked on the fawn-spotted leaves, but further wrote: "I have sometimes come upon a solitary specimen of this yellow lily growing beside a mossy stone where the sunshine fell full upon it. Its two leaves stand up like fawn's ears, and this feature, with its recurved petals, gives it an alert, wide-awake look."

Two early nicknames still with us are adder's-tongue and dog-tooth violet, both choices due to that "reckless fashion" of chris-

YELLOW TROUT LILY

tening New World plants with Old World names, which so provoked Mrs. William Starr Dana when she wrote about Cow-SLIP, in 1893. There is nothing about these lilies to suggest an adder's-tongue, but it obviously was the nickname for some European plant or other that seemed similar. Nor is there anything to suggest the teeth of a dog, and these flowers are lilies, not violets. However, there is a slim excuse for this seemingly irrelevant choice. A Eurasian variety of trout lily has dog-toothed roots (its early Latin name was *dens canis*), and the flower is violet, so dog-tooth violet became a catch-all English term for the entire family and was given to the American species when they were first discovered.

Bear all these names in mind if you are looking in a botanical index. Prof. Edgar T. Wherry's *Wild Flower Guide* lists dog-tooth violet and trout lily. Roger Tory Peterson's and Margaret McKenny's *A Field Guide to the Wildflowers* lists adder's-tongue and trout lily. H. W. Rickett's *Wild Flowers of America* lists only dog-tooth violet. L. H. Bailey's three volume *Cyclopedia of Horti-culture* only mentions adder's-tongue. Dropping back to the 1890's, Mrs. Dana's *How to Know the Wild Flowers* lists adder's-tongue and dog-tooth violet and in her text approves of fawn lily as "pretty and significant." Neltje Blanchan's *Nature's Garden*, 1901, gives adder's-tongue, dog-tooth violet, and trout lily, but dismisses fawn lily.

In the mountains of the northwest, where the richest assortment of these lilies is to be found—some with eight to sixteen flowers per stalk, the flowers two to four inches across—there are other nicknames to reckon with: avalanche lily, glacier lily, and chamise lily. This last refers to the thickets of chamiso, typical of the Sierras where this lily thrives; chamiso is a Spanish and Portuguese word for heather.

For one last etymological confusion, the scientific title for the genus of these lilies is an ill-advised choice plucked from the pages of Roman naturalists, as you will see in the following comment by Meehan.

The name of the genus is not well traced. Dr. Gray says, "*Erythoronium* is from *Erythros*, Greek for 'red," which is inappropriate as respects the American species." Prof. Wood seems of the same opinion. Dr. Darlington believes that the name was from "the purple stains on the leaves." Botanists do not always give the reasons for their names, and we are left to guess at them. The earlier ones delighted in adopting ancient appellations. *Erythronium* occurs in Pliny and Dioscorides, and some of the older botanists thought it had reference to this plant, and so retained it, though the plant referred to by the ancient writers was evidently used in dyeing, which the Dog-tooth Violet could not be . . . —THOMAS MEEHAN, *The Native Flowers and Ferns of the United States*, 1880

Even early in the season, while most of the tree leaves are still in the bud stage, the graceful yellow blossoms of Eastern Trout-lily, or Dogtooth-violet, appear on woodsy slopes where the sun comes strongly between the bare branches overhead. Rarely do you find it under evergreen trees, for this early spring opportunity to bask in the sun seems to be one of its requirements. Its flower usually close at night and they last for only a few days. By the end of May they, along with the curiously mottled leaves, have vanished. —ROBERT S. LEMMON and CHARLES C. JOHNSON, *Wildflowers of North America*, 1961

TUCKAHOE. See ARUM

VALERIAN—The name is synonymous with strong medicine and strong perfume, and it comes from *valere,* to be strong, in Latin. It's also been suggested that the name was given because this plant was said to have first been found in the Roman province belonging to the Valerius clan, so-called because of their strength—which brings us back again to *valere,* to be strong.

There are a number of valerians, but the European *valerian officinalis* that now grows wild in America, is that one that has figured in pharmacopedia over the centuries as a nerve tonic reputed to induce sleep where even opium has failed. "Valerian, calmer of hysteric squirms," wrote Dr. Oliver Wendell Holmes, and at the opening curtain of Chekhov's *The Anniversary,* an aged bank clerk rushes on stage, shouting, "Send someone to the chemist's for three pennyworth of valerian drops . . . I am utterly worn out. I feel ill all over." In America, in the 1800's, valerian was among the medicinal crops cultivated and sold by the Shakers; it "comforts the heart," wrote a contemporary herbalist. Dropping far back into ancient history, valerian was one of the seventy-two ingredients (including mashed vipers) that Mithradates brewed up for his famous antidote against poison—a recipe he researched paranoically, year after year, with poisoned slaves as his guinea pigs.

The Persians, Egyptians, and other Near Easterners were very keen on valerian as a perfume and spice, and it was *the* perfume in Europe in the Middle Ages—a heavy, almost overwhelming scent, which was perhaps very necessary in the bathless old days in dank castles. Cats go into frenzies at the smell of valerian, clawing it out of the ground and rolling in it with wild delight. Hence the old nickname, cat's fancy. At a distance, it's a tempting scent, rather like the vanilla-and-spice of heliotrope, and valerian is often called garden heliotrope though they are in no way related. But bury your nose in a clump of valerian or bring home a bouquet, and the scent is overwhelming—almost fetid.

We have a few native valerians in America, among them a western variety whose roots were steamed and stewed for food by the Digger Indians. The blue-flowered Jacob's-ladder (so called because of its parallel ladder-like leaves) is often called Greek valerian, though it's actually one of the phlox family. But there is a blue-flowered, ladder-leaved valerian in Europe, and the colonists presumably brought the name with them and used it over again for this American flower.

To Cure Fits. Put as much valerian root, and the castor or wart from a horse's leg, which is to be cleaned and cut into small pieces, as will be digested in a pint of whisky. Dose—three teaspoonfuls a day, and repeated until a cure is effected. A son of Mr. Hoyer's of Shelby, Niagara County, twelve years old, was subject to fits terribly, being in a fit sometimes for two hours. Dr. Failing, next town, obtained the above remedy in Canada, which cured the boy in six months.—D. MAGNER, *The New System*, 1883

Whenever, in driving about, I see a particularly fine plant in a dooryard, I make friends with its owner, and later suggest that if she (it usually is "she") will give me a small root of this or that, I will bring her some plants or bulbs from my garden, of a kind which she has not. So we are both equally benefited. In this way I was once given a plant of *Valerian*, which has a tall, beautiful white flower with a most delicious odour like vanilla. It blooms for three weeks in late May and early June. From this one plant there are now in the garden a number of large clumps several feet in diameter, and I have given away certainly fifty roots. Valerian is a small white flower in good-sized clusters on long stems, seen now-a-days only in old-fashioned gardens. I am told it cannot be bought of horticulturists.—HELENA RUTHERFURD ELY, *A Woman's Hardy Garden*, 1907

V E T C H comes from the Latin *vicia*, or vetch, which

comes from *vincire,* to bind, to twist—also the root word for PERI-
WINKLE. Vicia went into Old North French as *veche,* and moved
into English as vetch. And the vetches, a world-wide family, are
indeed binders and twisters, sending out a green veil of flowering
vines up and around and across whatever else is growing nearby.
We have an assortment of native varieties throughout the country and an equally wide-spread assortment of European imports
gone wild. Crown vetch, one of these imports, is a popular planting along new highway embankments and the like, where it holds
the raw soil and also serves as an attractive ground cover.

Tare, an alternate name, is a Middle English word that originally meant the seed of the vetch, rather than the whole plant,
as it does today. But this is not the tare of the Bible, which is a
kind of bearded grass with poisonous seeds that looks very much
like wheat and grows in wheatfields. Thus the parable about the
separation of the wheat from the tares, or the separation of the
good from the evil, in Matthew, XIII: 25–30.

July 6, 1851. Concord, Massachusetts . . . From the lane in front
of Hawthorne's, I see dense beds of tufted vetch, for some time,
taking the place of the grass in the low grounds, blue inclining in
spots to lilac like the lupines. . . . It is affecting to see such an
abundance of blueness in the grass. It affects the eyes, their celesial
color. I see it afar, in masses on the hill-sides near the meadow,

much blue, laid on with so heavy a hand.—HENRY DAVID
THOREAU, *Journals*

V I O L E T, like rose, has no translation. It is a variation
on *viola,* the early Latin name. And like the rose, violet became
the word for a color, though not all violets are violet. They bloom
in white, yellow, blue, magenta, and even green-brown. Some are
fragrant, some are not. Their variety is infinite. North America's
list of native violets is not only lengthy, but always incomplete,
because these flowers continually cross-breed in the wild. New
and pretty variations pop up everywhere throughout our woodlands.

The Greeks, and Milton, alike speak of violets as growing in
meadows or dales. But the Greeks did so because they could not
fancy any delight except in meadows; and Milton, because he
wanted a rhyme to nightingale—and was, after all, London bred.
But Viola's beloved knew where violets grew in Illyria—and grow
everywhere else also, when they can—on a *bank,* facing south. . . .
The reader must remember that he cannot know what violet colour
really is, unless he watch the flower in its *early* growth. It becomes
dim in age, and dark when it is gathered—at least, when it is tied
in bunches. At all events, no other single flower of the same quiet
colour lights up the ground near it as a violet will. A young violet
glows like painted glass.—JOHN RUSKIN, *Prosperina,* 1874

Under the great wind, on that early March morning, we drove
for miles over the wet prairie lands where the parade of spring
flowers had already begun . . . the blue of violets—the first violets of
our long trip. From the Kissimmee Prairie a tide of violets runs
north. In later weeks we saw them everywhere, high in the mountains, along the coast, edging the dark northern forests . . . like
the multitudinous footprints of spring, scattered over the map
before us.—EDWIN WAY TEALE, *North with the Spring,* 1965

V I P E R ' S B U G L O S S is an anathema to farmers and
was once nicknamed "blue devils." But it is a delight to the eye.

The flowers, fanned out on curving stalks, are crimson-pink when in bud and violet-blue when in bloom; the broad bristled leaves are a soft, silvery green. Because of the broad rough leaves, typical of the bugloss family, the Greeks gave the name, which means "ox-tongued," from *bouglossos*.

Once upon a time bugloss was also known as *Alcibiadion*, after Alcibiades, who was said to have discovered its use against snake-bite. The seeds are shaped like viper heads, and in ancient medical logic this was a sure indication that the plant was a specific for snake venom. Disocorides proclaimed its powers in the first century A.D., and so did a medical book printed in Exeter, New Hampshire, in 1824.

Viper's bugloss spread from its native Mediterranean home in centuries past—up through Europe, across the Channel to England, and during the late 1600's made its appearance in the Virginia Colony, possibly in a shipment of seed or in the hay and straw that was used to pack breakables. From Virginia it moved north through the Eastern states, headed west into Pennsylvania, and was last seen spreading through Kansas.

Bugloss is hot and moist, and therefore worthily reckoned up amongst those herbs which expel melancholy, and exhilarate the heart; an herb indeed of such sovereignty . . . that, if taken steept in wine, if wife and children, father and mother, brother and sister, and all thy dearest friends, should die before thy face, thou couldst not grieve or shed a tear for them.—Robert Burton, *Anatomy of Melancholy*, 1621

Continual eating of it makes the body invincible against the poyson of Serpents, Toads, Spiders, etc. The rich may make the Flowers into a conserve, and the herb into a syrup: the poor may keep it dry: both may keep it as a Jewell.—Nicholas Culpepper, *The English Physician Enlarged*, 1653

Another vast field of blue, ever living in my memory, was that of the Viper's Bugloss, which I viewed with surprise and delight from the platform of a train, returning from the Columbian Exposition [Chicago, 1893]; when I asked a friendly brakeman what the flower was called, he answered "Vilets," as nearly all workmen con-

fidently name every blue flower; and he sprang from the train while
the locomotive was swallowing water, and brought to me a great
armful of blueness. I am not wont to like new flowers as well as
my childhood's friends, but I found this new friend, the Viper's
Bugloss, a very welcome and pleasing acquaintance. Curious, too,
it is, with the red anthers exserted beyond the bright blue corolla,
giving the field, when the wind blew across it, a new aspect and
tint, something like a red and blue changeable silk. . . . It has
become in many states a tiresome weed . . . down the Hudson, acre
after acre of meadow and field by the waterside are vivid with its
changeable hues, and the New York farmers' fields are overrun by
the newcomer.—ALICE MORSE EARLE, *Old Time Gardens*, 1901

WAKE ROBIN. See TRILLIUM

WATER HEMLOCK, or Cowbane. See under
BANE.

WICKY. See under LAUREL

WILD BALSAM. See TOUCH-ME-NOT

WILD HYACINTH. See CAMASS

WISTERIA—The vines we usually find under cultivation are the Chinese and Japanese wisterias, with clusters of
lavish racemes, sometimes three feet long, the flowers white, pink,
or purple. The Oriental wisterias were the first ones to reach England, sent around 1725 by an officer of the East India Company
in Canton. The English nicknamed the vine "kidney-bean tree,"

LONG-CLUSTERED
AMERICAN WISTERIA

because of its seed pods, and for the scientific name they devised *Glycine frutescens,* or, the "sweet shrub." *Glycine* comes from the Greek *glykys,* or sweet, and is also the source for LICORICE.

Meanwhile, in the tangled, unexplored forests of our southern states, wild wisterias were twining and blooming amid the magnolias, the azaleas, and the dogwood. The first flower-hunters in North America gave our native wisteria the English choice of names with which they were familiar. When William Bartram journeyed down the Tallapoosa River in 1777 and described "spacious groves entangled with garlands," he listed the wild wisteria as *Glycine frutescens.*

There the matter rested until Thomas Nuttall came onto the American scene. An apprentice printer from Yorkshire, who settled in Philadelphia in 1808, Nuttall was introduced to the group of amateur and professional scientists who devoted themselves to the study of natural history. Botany became Nuttall's special interest, thanks to the influence of Dr. Benjamin Smith Barton (who also appears in the entries under Pogonia and Ginseng). Encouraged by his Philadelphia friends, Nuttall, a reclusive and solitary-minded man, took off alone on a plant collecting trip through Georgia and Mississippi and the Missouri River basin, and later along the Arkansas and Red Rivers. Upon his return, he published *The Genera of American Plants.* And it was Nuttall who gave American wisteria its name in 1818, in honor of Dr.

Casper Wistar, the Philadelphia physician and naturalist, who died that same year. (There are more biographical notes on Nuttall under KNAPWEED.)

In 1825, a Swiss botanist named De Candolle classified the kidney-bean tree, or *Glycine frutescens*, in the Nuttall genus of wisteria, thus bringing the Oriental and the American species into the same camp.

Doctor Caspar Wistar was a surgeon of high professional standing, and at the same time a man of highest social standing. He was also a man of most hospitable ways, and he gathered at his house, one evening in each week, numbers of his closest friends, with the understanding that any distinguished visitor from out of town was also to be brought by any of them. Wistar died in 1818, but so important had the parties become, as a social feature, that it was decided to continue them, and the club, known to this day as the Wistar Party, was formally organized. . . . The doctor is also remembered in one of the most charming of all possible ways, for there is named after him a vine which clambers up the front of myriads of houses in this and other cities, in this and other countries, one of the most beautiful of all flowering vines, delicately tossing to the breeze the pale purple of its plumes.—ROBERT SHACKLE-TON, *The Book of Philadelphia*, 1918

I sincerely hope it is still alive and will continue to live for many a year, the two-hundred-or-more-years-old despot, the incoercible, rampageous wisteria that spilled over the garden of the house where I was born and down into the Rue des Vignes. . . . The memories of my earliest childhood are embalmed with its full May flowering and its meagre second flowering in August–September. It used to be as heavy with bees as with bloom, creating a murmur like the reverberation of a cymbal that spread without fading away, more lovely each year, until the day when Sido, as she leaned in curiosity over its weight of flowers, let out the little 'Ah! Ah!' denoting a great discovery long anticipated: the wisteria had begun to uproot the railing.

As there could be no question, in Sido's domain, of destroying a wisteria, this giant continued to exercise . . . its deliberate strength. I saw it raise aloft and brandish a considerable length of railing torn from stone and mortar, twist the bars into a buckled imitation of its own contorted growth. . . . It happened that it came into contact with the neighboring honeysuckle . . . It affected at first not to have noticed this, then slowly strangled it as a snake suffocates a bird. I learned, by watching this take place, how murderous is the power employed by such convincing splendour.—COLETTE, *For a Flower Album*, 1949

W I T C H - H A Z E L has nothing whatsoever to do with witches, despite the plant's mystic knack as a divining rod for water and precious ores. The old name is quite prosaic, no magical spells here. Witch comes from *wych*, a variant of the Anglo-Saxon *wican*, to bend. (This is also the root word for wicker, which is woven from bendable or pliable branches.)

The name witch-hazel was given to the shrub because the leaves resembled those of the English elm tree with long, drooping branches that was known as the wych-elm; that is, "the bending elm." And the wych-elm was also called wych-hazel, because *its* leaves resembled those of the hazel tree. (The origins of elm and hazel, both Old English, are uncertain.) Over the years, "wych" was transformed into "witch." (The other kind of witch comes from the early English *wicca*, a wizard.)

The flowering shrubs we know as witch-hazel are native to America, Japan, and China, six species in all that bloom in fall, winter, or early spring, wreathing the leafless twigs with spidery blossoms. American witch-hazel was introduced to England in the 1690's, the Chinese in 1879.

The Indians had always cultivated witch-hazel for its medicinal value. A poultice from the inner bark cured eye diseases, and an extract of the bark soothed bruises and skin irritations, the use to which it is still put today.

I shall tell you what I learn'd of the use of the [witch hazel] from a Minister of the Church of England who officiates among the Mohawk Indians. He saw an allmost total blindness occasioned by a blow, cur'd by receiving the Warm Stream of a Decoction of the Bark of this Shrub through a Funnel upon the place. This was done by direction of a Mohawk Indian after other means had for a considerable time prov'd ineffectual. I have since experienc'd the benefit of it used in the same manner in an Inflammation of the eye from a blow.—*From a letter, 1744, by Dr. Cadwallader Colden, New York, to Prof. Johann Friedrich Gronovius, Leyden.*

Today, October 21st, I found the air in the bushy fields and lands under the woods loaded with the perfume of the witch-hazel —a sweetish, sickening odor. Nature says, "Postively the last." It is a kind of birth in death, of spring in fall, that impresses one as a little uncanny. All trees and shrubs form their flower-buds in the fall, and keep secret till spring. How comes the witch-hazel to be the one exception, and to celebrate its floral nuptials on the funeral day of its foliage? No doubt it will be found that the spirit of some lovelorn squaw has passed into this bush, and that this is why it blooms in the Indian summer rather than in the white man's spring. —JOHN BURROUGHS, *A Year in the Fields*, 1875

I shall never forget the thrill I had when I saw my first witch-hazel in bloom. It was a bitter day in early February, and I arrived at the cottage just as it was getting dark. . . . The witch-hazel was situated at the farthest end of the orchard wall. It was situated at the farthest end of the orchard wall. It was hardly worth while going to look at it, on a night like this. After all, I had watched it for weeks, there had never been a sign of life. The buds remained like cloves, apparently sealed with a seal that would not break until spring. Then I said to myself . . . go to the farthest corner of the orchard wall, see the witch-hazel, curse its barren twigs, and go in to have a drink. I went. And there, in the gathering darkness, with the high strange wind roaring through the great elm branches above me, I saw that the twigs of the witch hazel had broken into golden stars. It was a miracle . . . —BEVERLEY NICHOLS, *Down the Garden Path*, 1932

W O L F S B A N E. See under BANE

W O O D B E T O N Y. See BETONY

W O R M W O O D. See under ARTEMISIA

W O R T, a common suffix in so many of our plant names, is the present day English version of an early northern European word for any plant or herb, such as the Anglo-Saxon *wyrt,* the Old Norse *urt,* and the Old High German *wurz.*

Since wort is no longer a general term, it is prefixed with a descriptive word to indicate just which "wort" is under discussion. Ragwort has ragged leaves; bellwort, bell-shaped flowers; moneywort, coin-shaped leaves; spiderwort, long spider-legged leaves; and butterwort, the little insectivore, has buttery or oily leaves that attract insects and then curl around their prey to digest them. Mitrewort, or bishop's-cap, has mitre-like "caps" on the seed pods.

Feverwort cured fevers; woundwort, wounds; liverwort, liver ailments; cankerwort, canker sores; motherwort, uterine ailments; and thoroughwort supposedly cured almost everything. Pilewort cured piles, and figworts cured figs—fig being an obsolete English word for any swelling or protuberance, such as the lumps in the neck from tubercular lymph glands. Mugwort, from the Anglo-Saxon *mucg* or midge, repelled midges, fleas, flies, lice, and what-have-you. Lousewort, however, was believed to *cause* lice if eaten by sheep or cattle.

And there is soapwort, whose bruised leaves make a kind of soapy lather. Brought to America from England as one of the useful household herbs, it now blooms everywhere—pink, phlox-like flowers, happily surviving whether in a meadow or on the slopes of a gravel pit or the sidings of a railroad. Soapwort's other common name is bouncing bet, though no one seems to remember who Bet was. No more than they remember Susan of the black-eyed susans, or Johnny of the johnny-jump-ups.

Z E P H Y R   L I L Y. See Atamasco Lily

Z I N N I A—We have wild varieties of zinnia growing from southern Colorado down through New Mexico and Arizona. They are typically pale yellow or sulphur-colored, such as the desert zinnia of the southwest, a prickly hedgehog of a plant.

Southwards through Mexico to Brazil and Chile, wild zinnias bloom in more vivid colors and long before the Spanish conquest were cultivated in Aztec gardens. They were introduced to Europe in the 1700's and hybridized into the many double nursery varieties that we grow today. An early nickname was youth-and-old-age, because the old flowers stay fresh even as new flowers on the same stalk begin to bloom.

In *Garden Facts and Fancies* (1949), Alfred C. Hottes quotes a tale of the zinnias, entitled "Treasure that Bandits Reject." The story may be apochryphal, but here's the gist of it.

Early in the eighteenth century, a German botanist from the

PRAIRIE ZINNIA

University of Göttingen was exploring the mountains of Mexico for new plants, when he came upon a purple flower he had never seen before. It had just finished blooming, so that only a few flowers were at their best. He gathered a sack full of the faded ones, hoping that some would be sufficiently mature to have ripened seeds.

Suddenly, the German botanist was attacked by bandits. They seized his sack of treasure and were about to murder him, when the leader opened the sack to see what it contained. There was nothing in the sack but dead flowers. Who, but an idiot, would wander through the mountains with a sack of dead flowers? Since it was bad luck to murder the feeble-minded, the bandits let their prisoner go on his way.

Thus, the German botanist made his escape, returned to Europe with his new flower specimens, and Linnaeus gave the flowers his name. They are the zinnias, and the botanist was Dr. Johann Gottfried Zinn.

> The garden zinnia has only one palpable fault: it is unmistakably stiff. Yet, putting aside this little defect, we may certainly consider it a gifted flower. It has an astonishing range of color—white, buff, pale yellow, deep yellow, orange, light orange, scarlet, crimson, magenta, pure pink, lilac, purple, an intense deep red . . . and that delightfully subdued quality which we call crushed strawberry.
> —F. Schuyler Mathews, *Familiar Flowers of Field and Garden*, 1895

> The marvellously improved zinnias, some of whose lambent, glowing flowers look especially well in burnished copper bowls.
> —Neltje Blanchan, *The American Flower Garden*, 1909

> The idea of the useful still governs Florentine landscape architecture: the lemon trees in earthen tubs that flank the villas and then go into the *limonaiai,* or lemon house, for the winter, the long lines of cypresses, which act as wind-breaks. . . . Big pots of bright geraniums and daisies, bunches of zinnias—the quick growing flowers of the poor and the peasants—are the chief flowers of the Tuscan villas. Cut-and-come-again; how to make a little go a long way.
> —Mary McCarthy, *The Stones of Florence*, 1959

3 1166 00088 7226